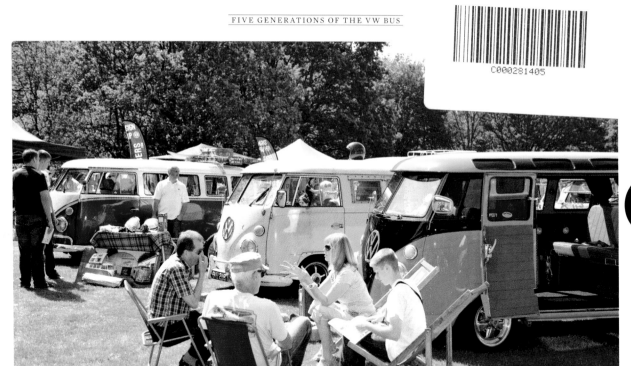

3

FROM THE PUBLISHERS OF

Jazz Publishing 1 Marcher Court, Sealand Road, Chester CH1 6BS
Tel:01244 881888   www.jazzpublishing.co.uk

EDITOR
Fergus McShane ☎ Ext. 224
fergus@jazzpublishing.co.uk

ART EDITOR
Gareth Evans ☎ Ext. 204
gareth@jazzpublishing.co.uk

DESIGNER
Owen Moran ☎ Ext. 202
owen.moran@jazzpublishing.co.uk

PRODUCTION MANAGER
Justine Hart ☎ Ext. 235
justine@jazzpublishing.co.uk

DIGITAL CONTENT
Gareth Williams ☎ Ext. 302
gareth.williams@jazzpublishing.co.uk

ADVERTISING MANAGER
Mark McCarthy ☎ Ext. 304
mark@jazzpublishing.co.uk

ADVERTISING SALES
Wendy Lennon ☎ Ext. 314
wendy.lennon@jazzpublishing.co.uk
Karen Hall ☎ Ext. 301
advertising@volkswagencamper.co.uk

ACCOUNTS & ADMIN MANAGER
Emma McCrindle ☎ Ext. 274
accounts@jazzpublishing.co.uk

ADMINISTRATION
Jan Schofield ☎ Ext. 219
jan@jazzpublishing.co.uk

CREDIT CONTROL
Pam Coleman ☎ Ext. 215
pam@jazzpublishing.co.uk

CIRCULATION & PROMOTIONS
Katy Cuffin ☎ Ext. 501
katy@jazzpublishing.co.uk

PUBLISHER
David Gamble
david@jazzpublishing.co.uk

MANAGING DIRECTOR
Stuart Mears
stuart@jazzpublishing.co.uk

The views expressed in this bookazine by the
contributors are not necessarily those of the
publishers. While every effort has been made
in compiling *Five Generations of the VW Bus*
the publishers cannot be held responsible for
any effects therefrom. Reproduction of any
matter contained in *Five Generations of the
VW Bus* is prohibited without prior permission.
Adverts and advertisers appearing in *Five
Generations of the VW Bus* carry no implied
recommendation from the bookazine or from
the publishers.

EDITORIAL

When we set out with a plan to compile a bookazine covering the iconic VW Transporter through all five generations, little did we know the difficulty we'd face in whittling down the hundreds upon hundreds of spectacular vans we've featured in Volkswagen Camper & Commercial and VW Bus T4&5+ over the years to a very select few. But whittle down we have—we hope you enjoy discovering the finished line-up. Thanks to all involved in the various stages of production—you know who you are— who helped this bookazine reach concours standard.

Fergus

Fergus McShane, *Editor*

COVER IMAGE: Simon Cooke

CONTRIBUTORS

David Eccles, Jon Robinson-Pratt, Simon Cooke, Dave Bowers, Dave Warren, David Hall, Cory McDowell, Nicky Connor, Damian Van Spall, Graham Snodden, Dave Richards, Stuart Thomas, Fleur & Kevin Challis, Alan Hayward, Grant Richards, James Whitlock, James Randle, Ian Garrad, James Northcott, Rick Davy, Mick Kok, Andrew Thompson, VW Press

CONTENTS

4

WELCOME...

🖥 : David Eccles

To this first VW bus, camper and commercial booka-zine! Designed to be an introduction the world of the iconic VW Transporter, inside you will find not only a concise overview of the key models and changes made to the five generations of the Transporter 1950–2014, but also guidelines as to how to set about buying the bus of your dreams, deciding which model or generation is best and advice on sourcing a bus and key things to bear in mind.

Importantly, it also showcases and celebrates some of the nicest buses around, from stunning stock, original examples to fully customised and modified versions. The five examples of each generation that grace these pages have previously been featured in VW Camper & Commercial magazine (founded 2001) or its sister publication VW Bus T4&5+ (founded 2011) but have been re-presented and brought together for you to admire and be inspired by. The hardest part of the job has been selecting which of the many stunning buses we have featured over the years to choose! We hope you are as pleased with the choices as we are!

Over 60 years after the humble, no frills VW 'box on wheels' was first introduced, the VW Transporter is now more popular than ever; both as a working commercial (which is what is was originally designed as) and as a lei-sure vehicle or camper. Quite why is difficult to explain, but no other vehicle engenders such warm affection or is so central to the lives of its owners. VW campers and buses now command very high prices and are highly sought after; they symbolise fun, freedom and adventure and are fre-quently used in advertising campaigns and films to project lifestyle images. With a VW bus or camper we tap into our psyche and need to be part of that romantic dream harking back to a time when life was much more simple. Whether the low-tech lifestyle of an old Split or Bay (which you can actually work on and learn to fix) or the modern driving

experience of a new T5, 'getting out in the bus' introduces us to new people, new friends, and new places. Although often associated with surfers or 'hippies', the truth is that VW owners are an eclectic mix of all ages and backgrounds who share a common passion—the love of their bus, whatever its generation.

The camper is, of course, the vehicle of choice. 'Home is where you park it!' sums up the thrill of being able to simply pack up and head off to the beach or the hills. Whether you drive a classic Westfalia camper or a bespoke all mod-cons T4 or 5, the feeling of being able to leave the stress of modern living behind for a while and get back to simpler things is essentially the same. I drove a '66 Split camper to India and back in 1976 and then owned the same '67 Devon Split Camper for 34 years. Nowadays I drive a modern T5 California; the driving and camping experiences may be different, but not the pleasure.

Owning a VW bus is about lifestyle, an essential part of which is built round socialising with family and friends, and meeting like-minded people who share the same passion. Many informal clubs and groups organise events and camp-outs, and there is a huge show scene offering everything from small informal one-day events to full-on, packed with entertainment weekends. Bus festivals such as Camper Jam or Busfest bring the whole community together—10,000+ VW buses with their families all sharing in the vibe. Many tribes; one nation.

Drive your bus; enjoy your bus

David.

David Eccles
Editor VW Camper & Commercial magazine

This brochure image shows the full range of T1 factory models including high roofs and pick-ups.

THE BIRTH OF A
LEGEND

The T1, aka Splitscreen, Split, or Bulli: 1950–67

🚐 : *David Eccles*

The origin of the no frills Transporter lies in the need for lightweight commercial delivery vans, paramount in the post-WWII years. The bombed out VW factory in Wolfsburg—under the guidance of Major Ivan Hirst from REME—had restarted production of the VW Beetle and had even built its own flatbed load haulers, called Plattenwagens, to move items around the plant. Seeing them in action, Dutch importer Ben Pon tried to get permission to import them; a plan that the Dutch authorities rejected on safety grounds.

But Pon had not given up on the idea of a simple delivery van, and on a visit to the factory in 1947 he produced the famous sketch that inspired the shape and design of the VW

Transporter—a rounded front, driver seated up front over the wheels, load space in the middle and engine at the rear. The idea was turned down, however, with Beetle production deemed the priority.

By 1948 the British Army had relinquished control of the factory and Heinz Nordhoff took over as MD. He resurrected the idea and in 1949 several prototypes, modelled on Ben Pon's original concept, were built and tested. The new Transporter was unveiled in March 1949, and full production commenced on March 8, 1950.

Initially only available as a panel van, in May 1950 the Microbus and Kombi models were introduced. The Kombi featured basic trim and removable seats—the first MPV! The

The Deluxe Microbus (Samba) has a sunroof, skylights and chrome trim. Pre-1963 versions also had rear corner windows.

1955–1963 models can easily be identified by the narrow tailgate and small back window.

Deluxe Microbus (aka Samba), with corner windows, sliding sunroof, roof windows and chrome trim came along in June 1951, an ambulance in November 1951, and the single cab pick-up truck in 1952. Apart from special body conversions the only other factory models were the double cab pick-up and the high roof models, introduced in 1958 and 1961 respectively. There were three key body styles until the end of T1 production, easily recognised and known as Barndoor buses, small back window buses and large back window buses.

Barndoor buses 1950–1955
One of the most distinctive features of pre-March 1955 buses is the large engine lid, which has given rise to the nickname Barndoor bus. There is also no overhang above the cab roof for fresh air ventilation. The Deluxe Microbus was the only model to feature a full-width dashboard and all buses ran on 16-inch wheels. Initially they were fitted with 1131cc (25hp) engines which were uprated in late 1953 to 1192cc (30hp).

Small back window buses 1955–1963
The new post-1955 models featured many upgrades and changes: the engine lid was made smaller; the fuel filler was now accessed by a side flap in the body; the tailgate was enlarged and fitted with a T handle; and the front overcab now had a peak to allow fresh air ventilation. All models now had a redesigned full dash with ashtray and provision for a radio, as well as quirky Barndoor features like the three-spoke steering wheel replaced with a two-spoke version. All models now ran on 15-inch wheels.

The new Transporter was unveiled in March 1949; full production commenced on March 8, 1950

Large back window buses 1963–1967
August 1963 saw another slight body change with a wider tailgate and bigger window in the rear and 'fish eye' front indicator lenses instead of 'bullet' style. Due to the enlarged tailgate the Deluxe model could no longer be fitted with corner windows at the rear. The new optional 1500cc engine became standard in late 1964 and uprated to 44hp in 1965. 12v electrics arrived in August 1966.

Camping conversions
Westfalia was amongst the first to provide a camping conversion for the Transporter, launching a removable kit called the Camping Box in 1953. By 1955, however, Westfalia also produced a fully fitted camper featuring an opening roof hatch. In 1959 SO 23 was introduced and set the pattern for future Westfalia styling with wood panelled roof and walls, plaid upholstery, and even a 'cocktail' cabinet. In 1963 SO 34 was introduced, commonly known as a 'Flipseat' model due to the cab seat back which could rotate to form L-shaped seating in the rear. This was superseded by SO 42 in 1965, which featured a pop-top roof.

In Britain the market was dominated by the three Ds... Devon, Dormobile and Danbury. Devon was the first production line UK-built camper in 1957, Canterbury Pitt from 1959, Dormobile from 1961, and Danbury from 1964.

Production of the T1 Splitscreen continued until July 1967, with a total of 2.3 million selling worldwide. ●

10

BARNDOOR
BARN
FIND

Since its introduction in June 1951 the Deluxe Microbus, affectionately known as a Samba, has been seen as a jewel in the crown of VW buses

📷 : Jon Robinson-Pratt 🖥 : David Eccles

Rolling off the production line in 1953, this Samba is beautifully finished in the classic Deluxe colours of Chestnut Brown over Sealing Wax Red. With a mix of early and later Barndoor features and being built in March this version would have been one of the first VW bus models to be fitted with a rear bumper (introduced for the Deluxe in March 1953, but not on other models till December) and also featured the new style of smooth semaphores and domed rear light lenses. »

Bought new from Volkswagen in Portugal, the bus passed down from generation to generation before it found itself stored away in a garage for 25 years

The new design pivoting quarter lights, downward angled mirror arms and narrower accelerator pedal were also new styling features introduced in January '53, but the old style of backwards reading speedo is still standard as this was not updated with a conventional version till December, when

other features such as a combined ignition/starter switch, interior light with door contacts, and painted wiper arms were introduced.

There are also some unusual and quite rare factory options on this version; notably the Petite Bat Wing Horn Ring and the dashboard Becker Radio. Also fitted from new were the roof rack and the ultra-rare skylight window Venetian blinds—an item most will never have seen before!

Bought new from Volkswagen in Portugal, the bus passed down from generation to generation before it found itself stored away in a garage for 25

years until it was unearthed by Gavin Harverson—owner of Southwestsplitz. Happening upon a website advert offering a '1953 eight-seater VW' and expecting to find a more regular Kombi, upon seeing pictures of the Deluxe Microbus features a rescue mission to portugal was quickly underway. Two days of travelling later and the Samba was winched free from the shed, dusted off and strapped down ready for the drive back to Britain where the long task of washing, cleaning and getting her roadworthy again could begin.

Having been repainted in the late '70s before being stored away, although it no longer sports the desirable original paint/patina, it has stood the test of time and dust well. Paintwork aside the bus was still essentially stock with its six-leg middle seat, five matching 16-inch rims, original 1200cc gearbox, and later 1200cc engine fitted. Due to the bus being off the road for so long the brakes were all seized on and all cylinders were in bad shape necessitating the fitting of new brakes throughout. Then after driving her around for a year or so Gav realised that trying to keep up with traffic with a 1200cc was not really practical and a bit more HP »

14

"The bus works well for us as a family at the moment and the kids love going out for day trips in her. Driving and owning such a rare bus is a real buzz and every time I take my family out in her it puts a smile on my face." *Gav Harverson*

was needed! The bus now sports a 2.4 Stroker motor with Rancho gearbox, 48 Webber carbs and full flow oil system with external oil cooler; CSP disc brakes with dual master cylinder and larger Type 3 rear brakes have been fitted to cope with the power increase. A 12v conversion has also uprated the bus for modern driving conditions. Period '50s cool box BBQ and suitcases complete the vintage look inside.

Since getting back on the road, the bus has been used for family day trips. The interior remains basically original, although Gav has plans to carry out a full restoration at some point, including replacing the interior panels with original style versions. However there are no plans to 'camperise' the interior—no, this is to remain a very rare and original bus. ●

LUCKY
THIRTEEN

Winning Best in Show and Best Split at Devon Dubfest; Best Split at Dubs in the Castle; and Best Interior at the 2013 Cornwall Jamboree, Dusty Millar's Split is a bus with pedigree

📷 🎞 : *Simon Cooke*

Named 'Lucky' because the 13-window model mirrors the fact that both Dusty and his son were born on Friday the 13th, Dusty purchased this, his first Split, back in 2008. Located and bought from the USA for £12,000, this 1965 Split was decidedly ratty on arrival, without floors front and back and with all sills needing replaced. But a project bus is what was wanted and this Split was perfect.

Still running the original 1500 single port engine, after a service it was good as new; for safety an automatic fire extinguisher system in the engine bay has been installed... just in case! And if anything major should go wrong the plan is to upgrade to a two-litre lump—mainly to help tow the teardrop caravan housing all his cooking and camping equipment that allowed Dusty to keep the Split as a day van. Mind you, unless he's actually away for a weekend there's no sign of him towing anything; it's all very stealth, as he explained: "I didn't want to change the look of the back but I did need it to be practical because I've got a family »

of five. It was quite hard to source my hidden tow bar." It's certainly discreet and hard to spot unless it's pointed out.

The body work, carried out by Anthony at Autostyl, was essentially a bare metal restoration. Amazingly, all the original panels were retained except for one of the rear quarters, although it's obviously had new floors and sills fitted. And to finish the exterior in style, Dusty had the van finished in a new colour combination of Alpine White and Valiant Green. Underneath, the van has been treated to a new wiring loom, Porsche 944 discs on the front, the original drums on the rear, with a set of 15-inch Porsche replica Fuchs alloys to roll on. The entire van has also been lowered 3.5 inches. Parts that were refurbished and used again include the Deluxe clock, dashboard

instruments, steering box and reduction boxes. Open the side doors and you'll see all the items (colour co-ordinated) you expect from an award-winning van—wooden floor, handmade table, handmade curtains, full-width rock & roll bed and rear-facing bench seat. But there're also a couple of nice exclusive touches which you don't see everywhere. Following on from the hidden tow bar, a stealth TV has also been installed. Inspired by a visit to a bed shop where he saw a TV pop up from the end of a bed, Dusty had a 24-inch TV installed on actuators allowing it to rise from the back of the seating area—ideal for keeping the kids amused during long journeys.

Continuing the stealth theme up front, an original ash trash for the dashboard has been updated with a hidden iPod dock that connects to

All the original panels were retained except for one of the rear quarters, although it's obviously had new floors and sills fitted

This Split, like many projects, took longer than expected and ran over the £22,000 budget set, but it has definitely been worth all the time, effort and money that's gone into it

his ICE system with retro digital stereo without having to cut the dash... result.

Finally hitting the open road in August 2012, this Split, like many projects, took longer than expected and ran over the £22,000 budget set, but it has definitely been worth all the time, effort and money that's gone into it. Dusty is rightfully proud of his van, with the only regret being that he

doesn't get behind the wheel as often as he'd like—working offshore means spending weeks away, so Dusty makes up for it by driving his Split at every opportunity when he's home, including popping to the shops, gym, and even doing the school run.

In 2014 the entire family are embarking on a tour of Europe so they can spend some proper quality time with Lucky, living the dream. ●

DRAG
DELUXE

Don't get the wrong impression from the rat style of this Split—there's a sting in the tail that guarantees fast times at the Santa Pod quarter-mile

📷🖥 : *Dave Bowers*

What first attracted Chris Byron to this van was its distinctive patina formed from standing outside in a field for 22 years. Imported by the previous owner who had made some improvements, Chris had his own ideas when it came to finishing his drag bus—the bodywork provided the dissolute rat-look, while the work on the brakes and suspension was the base for blistering performance once a powerful engine was added.

The front suspension was lowered using a TransporterHaus six-inch narrowed front beam with a set of dropped spindles. The steering was uprated by fitting a Creative-Engineering rack conversion. For the front brakes, Chris installed a set of AirKewld Bad discs, with the discs kitted out with Wilwood four-pot callipers. At the rear, a straight axle conversion with adjustable spring plates worked well, with the transaxle choice settling on a Rancho Pro-Comp item with a Rhino casing, and a set of Cromo, half-shaft, race-spec axles. The rear disc brakes are also AirKewld Bad, »

Throughout the build Chris made sure any components he chose would endure the 200bhp strain the engine would deliver once completed

but unlike the front brakes, these are worked by a single, standard VW, brake piston. Throughout the build Chris made sure any components he chose would endure the 200bhp strain the engine would deliver once completed!

Chris' wheel choice were a non-beadlock BTR set he imported from USA—and he's now the official UK supplier. Emulating the iconic dragster look of small wheels and a narrow front track at the front and larger wheels with a normal width track at the back was achieved by fitting narrow 4x15-inch BTR wheels on the front axle, and 7x15-inch BTR on the back. Tyres were chosen with road and drag use in mind; Bridgestone of 145x60mm at the front, and 225x60mm out back. The rear suspension was

set up with a hint of negative camber that's instantly cancelled out by a touch of throttle as the engine power's transmitted to the wheels.

An area of the rear cargo floor was cut out to improve engine access, with a T3 engine inspection cover neatly fitted in place, which also provides a bird's-eye view of the engine, shrouded by a Porsche-style Bernie Bergman cooling system fan housing sprayed in candy-apple metal flake.

Arriving at the engine, there's much too much »

minutiae to delve into in the space available here, but needless to say, Chris has created a machine that is entirely unique and tailor-made for hitting the drag strip quarter-mile, with an output now of over 200bhp in a classic Split! A list of some of the touches added include: lightweight parts (pistons, etc.) used where possible; carbs that give a controlled and progressive fuel feed; a lightning-quick ignition system; a rev limiter that cuts out at 6,000rpm so nothing goes bang, with a second stage limiter push button that keeps the engine primed for a launch start; and a bespoke dry sump system from CB Performance that carries eight litres of oil to cool the engine.

While a number of of bodywork repairs were made—offside sills, a few outriggers and front wheel arches replaced—the distressed rat-style was retained with any visible signs of corrosion underlining the scruffy, down-at-heel appearance. Adding a touch of something that smacks of being bizarre in the extreme, a Cyclop's eye headlamp sourced from a 1930s Chevy was added to the leading edge of the van's roof. Truck-style mini mirrors were fitted to the door pillars that add to the American look, which is further emphasised by the mock Alabama number plates and the Confederate

The bodywork provided the dissolute rat-look, while the work on the brakes and suspension was the base for blistering performance once a powerful engine was added

seat covers that hark back to where the van resided before being shipped to the UK.

Interior appointments include a set of rear seat units in timber and MDF that converts into a double bed. The van's interior was decorated with pages from old Eagle comics of the '60s for a touch of nostalgia. Cab improvements include a set of TMI vinyl seat covers and a BugTech shifter. Sunpro provided a rev counter, oil temperature and oil pressure gauge, and a fuel gauge on the opposite side of the dash. The design of the steering wheel with a set of holes around the periphery is based on ones fitted to midget hot-rods in the States, comple-

Achieving balance between ultimate power for a fast, dragstrip getaway, whilst ensuring the van remained road usable always entails a degree of compromise

mented by a boss sculpted out of a solid billet of aluminium, with the base being an oddity fabricated from a measuring jug. Finishing detail to meet drag racing regulations, a set of TRS four-point racing harnesses were fitted.

Achieving the right balance between ultimate power for a fast, dragstrip getaway, whilst ensuring the van remained road usable always entails a degree of compromise. This came in the shape of a less aggressive clutch set-up that now allows the van to pull away smoothly and progressively from just 500rpm, meaning Chris can be as comfortable driving to the drag strip as he is speeding down it! ●

A TWIST OF
DEVON

When a bus scoops all the awards at the SSVC AGM, including Restoration of the Year, Best Interior, Best Paint, and the coveted Van of the Year, then you know it has to be something rather special

📷 : *Dave Warren* 🚐 : *David Eccles*

A stunning, essentially stock 1956 Wolfsburg-built Split with quirky and attractive period features, it's the work quality, attention to detail, and of course, that handbuilt early Devon style oak interior that sets this bus above others.

On the lookout for a VW project in 2011, new owner, John Taylor Cox, found a rusting 1956 Kombi for sale in Cyprus on TheSamba.com; it looked to be the perfect base and was soon en route to Matt Smith's Cornwall shop for metalwork.

A RHD model produced at Wolfsburg in April 1956—which vary slightly from Hannover models » of the same period—the bus was stripped down to the shell, with John taking all the mechanics, running gear, etc., back to Jersey for refurbishment, whilst Matt set to on the body. As well as all the usual suspect areas needing attention, accident damage meant a donor roof from a '57 model was sourced, which had the added bonus of a factory Golde sunroof option.

With bodywork complete, the 1955/58 Microbus colour scheme of Palm Green over Sand Green was selected and applied, and the painted shell arrived back in Jersey in December 2012 for John to start work by first adding the two traditional body pinstripes to complete the exterior. Meanwhile the 1200cc engine, gearbox, front beam and running gear were carefully dismantled, meticulously cleaned or replaced without modification. No, this was to remain a stock bus. Additionally, just about every bit of the bus, including electrics and wiring, has been painstakingly refurbished or replaced using NOS parts wherever necessary.

While refurbishing the sunroof mechanism, frame, and fitting the canvas cover is an impressive feat in itself, John also did the headlining, before calling upon J&S Upholstery to trim the front seats and interior panels in leather, before fitting. John also replaced the two-spoke steering wheel

> Just about every bit of the bus, including electrics and wiring, has been painstakingly refurbished or replaced using NOS parts wherever necessary

with a Barndoor three-spoke version as "a concession to styling".

With the bus coming together nicely, John's mind turned to the interior. Inspired by photos of the curved side cabinet in early Devons, and armed only with pictures and some measurements from owners on the SSVC forum, he set about designing and building his own version using solid oak and oak veneered panels. Whilst he kept the key features of an early Devon with gas light, curved side cabinet, slope-fronted Osokool cabinet by the load door and dinette style bench seating, John has drawn on later Devon styling especially in the rear, which features slide-out drawers on the rear deck (also accessible from the interior) and enclosed storage cupboards, roof cupboard

The bus had its maiden adventure in 2014, when it took an epic trip from Jersey to the UK and up to Dover and thence to the Ben Pon Meet in Amersfoort

and hanging space. There is also an interior light above the side windows. The table is also an updated version of an early Devon one, the front leg mirroring the original shaped wood version but with two folding legs at the rear allowing the table to be used outside. The period 'gas' lamp found online had wiring threaded through it and a small bulb holder fitted to take a modern LED bulb. A small pull switch is hidden behind the mounting plate.

The finishing period touch comes from the Devon style flecked cushion cover fabric, which is a very close match to the original, and in green complements the exterior perfectly; the covers were made up by a local upholsterer, Josh. John found the curtain material, printed on both sides, again via the internet, and then made the curtains himself, incorporating magnets to hold them against the bottom of the windows and in the ends of the tie backs. All in all, the end result of the work that has gone into this bus is simply stunning.

The bus had its maiden adventure in April 2014, when it took an epic trip from Jersey to the UK and up to Dover and thence to the Ben Pon Meet in Amersfoort. And it performed faultlessly! Then in May John brought it over to the SSVC's annual big get together, where everyone who saw it was in awe of the workmanship and finished result. John's bus went on to win every award going and proudly led the convoy of over 200 Splits to Stanford Hall the next day. And as for the future, he says, "I just want to enjoy using it!" ●

RAISING
THE
ROOF

Lovingly restored to stock, this 1967 high roof delivery van is one of the finest examples of this rare model around

📷🖥 : *David Eccles*

VW introduced the Grossraum-Kastenwagen (large space delivery van) in September 1961, and it quickly established itself as the preferred option for businesses and mobile shops needing the extra headroom—not only could shop assistants stand up inside, but there was space for shelving, racks and rails too.

Like the crew cab, the model came about through customer demand, and though some versions had been produced in the '50s with fibreglass tops, VW's own factory model featured full-size metal body panels. These new full-height body and corner panels had to be created, along with a »

KON 918E

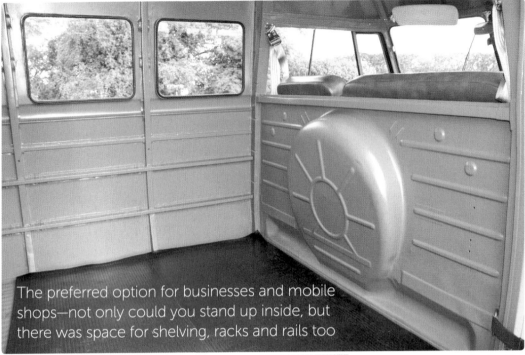

The preferred option for businesses and mobile shops—not only could you stand up inside, but there was space for shelving, racks and rails too

new curved panel above the windscreen. The upper cooling vents, fresh air intake and roof guttering were repositioned at the top of the raised roof bodyline, but the guttering above the windscreen was retained to help keep the screen clear in rain, as well as the guttering above the rear hatch. Originally based on the small tailgate (pre-1963) models, the narrow tailgate remained in place when the new wide tailgate version was introduced to maintain stability and roof strength. A sliding cargo door was found impractical for the same reasons, so new full-height cargo doors lined with metal to add rigidity were fabricated. Another version featuring an opening sales hatch was also available, and used by Westfalia for its SO2 Mobile Shop conversion.

This particular bus, now owned by Darren and Sarah Yip, was built in 1967 and finished in Light Grey. It was ordered by VW Portugal and featured factory options of safari windscreens, a larger oil bath air cleaner, and an engine with recessed pistons for low octane fuel—features often specified for vehicles exported to Portugal. In order to get round import duties, VW Portugal also fitted the two original factory windows seen on each side. It was first bought by a chemical company before

eventually passing on to a couple who converted it to a camper, adding a shower, two cookers, underslung water tank, and cutting out the front bulkhead to make a walkthrough cab.

The inspiration behind Darren's decision to purchase this model came from Sarah, who was fed up of having to bend over in their Devon tin top. It needed a lot of work doing, but Darren could see its quality would come through once returned to its former stock glory, wherever possible using original or NOS parts for the restoration. Spending nearly five years collecting and sourcing parts, in 2010 the stripped shell was finally trailered to

Matt Smith in Cornwall. The brief was simple—return it back to how it looked when it left the factory and what a job he has done!

The work took nearly 18 months and included new lower panels and sills, new cargo floor, new cab corners, and repairs to every window aperture. Unable to source an original high roof model tailgate, the original was reworked using a rust-free lower half grafted onto the upper section to obtain the correct profile. Likewise, sourcing NOS or rust-free high cargo doors was impossible, so these were repaired and new inner metal skins and interior panels (as originally fitted) fabricated »

The bus was awarded Van of the Year, Restoration of the Year, and scooped a Best Paint award

and fitted in place. Though a NOS engine lid was a real find! After working on any bits of rust or holes, the interior was painted in Dove Grey as per the factory spec, while the exterior was prepped and painted Dove Blue. The original 14-inch wheels were powdercoated black, then sprayed Silver White, and new hubcaps painted grey for the commercial look. NOS American-spec bumpers with over-riders were fitted, while a white painted front badge (NOS, of course) adds period custom style.

Once Darren collected the painted shell the bus was reassembled, including wiring, electrics, etc., over many long hours. Collecting parts being a passion of Darren's, on his finished bus the list is long and includes NOS handles, front and rear lights (RHD versions), black steering wheel, '67 only rubber knobs, 12v switches, and a radio blanking plate. The original speedometer and 12v petrol gauge were refurbished by Peter Banks. The cab bench/single seats were recovered in original-style mesh grey using TMI fabric, with new black rubber cab and cargo floor mats adding to the authentic look.

Engine-wise little needed to be done—the original 1500 engine was checked over and now purrs along, while the original gearbox and reduction boxes still perform perfectly to provide a smooth ride!

At its first show outing—the SSVC AGM event—the bus was awarded Van of the Year, Restoration of the Year, and scooped a Best Paint award. A fitting recognition of the time, love and effort that has gone into re-creating this classic commercial in true stock style. ●

Early Bays, built 1967–72, had low indicators, a large VW badge, and integral step in the bumper, as evidenced on this 1971 Westfalia.

36

A NEW
SHAPE

The T2, aka Bay window bus: 1967–1979

🏛 : *David Eccles*

T2a: Early Bay 1967–1972

Work began on completely re-designing the Transporter in 1964/5. It soon became apparent that a new approach to the body was needed, resulting in an extra skin to make the body self-supporting. The main external change was to have a one piece wrap-around front window (hence the Bay window name), one piece cab wind-down windows, and long side windows for a more contemporary look. The wheelbase remained the same, but the length increased by 160mm meaning the load area could now carry five cubic metres instead of 4.8. Reduction boxes were out and replaced with a new double jointed rear axle with semi-

trailing arms. A sliding side door, previously only available as an option, was now standard, and the opening access enlarged. Other upgrades and changes included relocating the engine cooling air vents to the upper rear of the body, providing more efficient cooling for the new 1570cc engine.

In 1971 disc front brakes were introduced, a 1700 Type 4 engine became available, and the rear end received a new rectangular tail light cluster and squarer shaped rear cooling vents. Buses built from August 1971 to August 1972 are often known as Crossovers as they retained the old style front end with low front indicators and rounded bumpers with an integral cab step in the front one, but had the redesigned rear end.

This fully original 1974 (Late Bay) Westfalia is a RHD Continental model.

Bespoke interiors allow owners to put their own stamp upon a bus.

T2b: Late Bay 1972–1979

In August 1972 the front end was also modernised. The indicators were moved to a more prominent position on either side of the front grill, the VW front badge was made smaller, and the bumpers were now square shaped with a step for the cab now integrated into the body. An automatic gearbox option was introduced in 1973 and the Type 4 engine uprated to 1800cc in 1974, with a fuel injected two-litre version, as fitted to the Porsche 914, available from 1975. Production of the new T3 model commenced in May 1979, but Bays continued to be produced in tandem until October 1979.

Brazilian Bays

Brazil continued manufacturing a version of the Bay, and from 1979 made their own version of the T2, which mixed body and other components from the T1 and the T2—essentially with twin opening side cargo doors, a Split rear end and a Bay front end. In 1997 VW Brazil introduced a restyled Bay with a slightly raised roof and mouldings on the cab doors, and in 2005 1.4-litre water-cooled versions replaced the old air-cooled engines, necessitating the siting of an extra grill at the front for the radiator cooling. Production of the T2 Brazilian Bay ceased on December 13, 2013, before which time VWB had produced 1.5 million T1/T2 Transporters.

Bay campers

Westfalia continued to lead the way and dominated the market, selling especially well in the USA. By the early '70s the factory was producing 135 units a day and 30,000 units annually, with 75 percent of these going to America! The new Bay campers went

Westfalia continued to lead the way and dominated the market, especially in the USA

on sale in January 1968 with either a pop-top, Dormobile roof, or Westfalia's new front-hinged version complete with twin bunks. This was changed to a rear-hinged version in 1973. In 1972 the first RHD production line Westfalia's were marketed in the UK as The Continental. Like the Split predecessors the various interior configurations over the years all carried an SO number showing the model's layout and equipment, though US versions were generically known as Campmobiles.

Devon continued to be the best selling UK camper, with models like the Caravette, Torvette, Moonraker and Devonette. In 1972 Devon was awarded exclusive rights from VW, giving their models access to the full VW dealer network and warranty. Named the Caravette, it was marketed by VW alongside the Westfalia Continental, but differed in that it combined people carrier and camper abilities. This arrangement continued until 1978 when Devon launched its Moonraker range, probably their most successful and influential layout of all. Dormobile continued to produce campers but ceased trading in the late '70s. New players included Viking (with a huge roof, sleeping space for three and featuring an overhanging tent extension) and Holdsworth (with an aluminium sided pop-top roof), as well as Bilbo's and Autosleeper, who are still going strong.

The Bay window model was VW's biggest selling Transporter model, with 3.9 million units produced over its 12-year life span. ●

WELCOME TO
HELSINKI

Paul and Bruce had long
enjoyed seeking refuge from the
day-to-day grind with camping
escapes. But were they ready to
take the next step?

📷 : David Hall 🖳 : Cory McDowell

Following the path of many, it took one too many frustrating setting up camp sessions next to a relaxed campervan scene that made Paul and Bruce finally realise they needed a camper. First looking beyond VWs in an effort to cover all the bases, after settling on a VW and doing some research, the decision was made to look out for a later Bay due to the larger engine, confirmed by an impressive YouTube walkthrough showing »

40

The interior really is in excellent condition considering its age, standing almost exactly as it left the factory back in '77 and is kept in pristine condition by the pair

the interior design and practicality of a Westfalia Helsinki conversion.

After a prolonged search, Paul and Bruce finally purchased their first VW in July 2011 from VW Kampers Limited based in Henfield, West Sussex, who seemed to be one of the only specialist providers offering a 12-month mechanical warranty on their vehicles. A combination of typical mechanical inexperience coupled with the fact that they were purchasing a 35-year-old vehicle made this a very appealing selling point! Upon arrival, they found a few Jaffa orange campers, one of which was ready for sale, but there was a particular green T2 in stock (not quite complete) far too attractive to overlook. The green perfectly embodied the 1970s nostalgia that they were looking for and they were amazed by the interior—although it did need a few bits replacing and a good clean to keep the judges on the concourse happy, but that was it! The icing

on the cake was the paintwork. It was almost flawless, with just a few spots of surface rust here and there. All told, it was in great shape.

The boys' Westy came with some documented history showing the T2 had been first registered in the UK in February 2002 and had had a couple of »

previous owners. There were also receipts show-ing substantial maintenance work over the years to keep it roadworthy, but as far as they could make out, the Westy has never undergone a full restora-tion... so this beautiful Helsinki is a true original.

Thus, in 2011 the guys at VW Kampers made the already great looking bus perfect by treating it to a full respray, and also fitted a new roof canvas with matching headliners, door cards and cab carpet, even the electric hook-up received the detailing treatment. They also replaced the heat exchangers and lowered the van by an inch or two; not for aesthetic purposes, they actually quite like the stock ride height. And neither did the pair use the usual excuse of 'improving handling'. No, this lowering job is for purely practical reasons... they just had to be able to fit the bus in the garage for insurance purposes.

Mechanically speaking, it's pretty much been plain sailing with the Helsinki; only returning to VW Kampers on the odd occasion for basic repairs, including fitting a new alternator and windscreen wiper motor. The guys love the fact that their bus is so original. The interior really is in excellent condi-tion considering its age, standing almost exactly as it left the factory back in '77 and is kept in pristine condition by the pair. That said, they bought it to use it, which means no cotton wool or bubble wrap for this bus either. Yes, it's got a few dents and dings as a result, but we think that only adds character.

One cool accessory is the original Westfalia box stool the guys acquired and had re-trimmed in matching green plaid, and they've also had identi-

The icing on the cake was the paintwork. It was almost flawless, with just a few spots of surface rust here and there. All told, it was in great shape

42

Paul and Bruce bought their Bay to use it, which means no cotton wool or bubble wrap for this bus either. Yes, it's got a few dents and dings as a result, but we think that only adds character

cal dash and rear mats trimmed to their own custom specifications. The three-way fridge is also the original unit and works on both 240 and the 12-volt supply, while the Trumatic-S gas heater is completely original, albeit needing fixed for when it gets cold.

"We have already been on many weekends and holidays away," said Paul, "including a couple of two-week trips to central and southwest France. The freedom of being able to throw in a few bits and bobs on a Friday evening and then set off on an adventure for the weekend is fantastic." We like this T2, and its owners. Not only is it wonderfully original, it resonates as a memento to a simpler time. It hasn't cost the owners the deposit for two houses, it doesn't take over their lives, and they don't need a mechanics degree to drive it. Paul and Bruce are more than happy travelling to their destinations at just the right pace to soak up the experience, and that is exactly how classic VWs should be enjoyed. ●

EARLY BAY
BEAUTY

Here comes Dylan! A gorgeous 1968 Westfalia
Bay with a big personality that's become a huge
part of his family's lives

📷 🎙 : *Nicky Connor*

Owners, Dan and Claire, had always wanted a bus as a way to escape from the rat race. After finding and restoring Dylan they got both of those and much, much more. "Since buying the bus all those years ago," Dan recalls, "we have made so many good friends, and the escapism it gives us has made everything worthwhile. We only wish we'd bought one sooner!"

Being massive VW fans for a long time, the pair wanted to get more involved with the lifestyle, and following a life-changing chat on whether to move house or buy a bus, they embarked on the journey of finding and converting Dylan into the beautiful Bay he is today.

Deciding that rather than buying an existing, running bus, they wanted to find a shell to restore to their own specifications, the pair travelled many miles and looked at many projects. After much searching they started to become a little disillusioned with the whole process—some garages were unhelpful and many buses they saw were not up to scratch but were very overpriced. Finally they found a garage in Oswestry with several buses on site—they fell in love with the bare shell of an Early Bay Type 2 Westfalia. A Californian import, it had little rust and was very straight with no signs of previous damage. It had been built in February 1968 as a Pearl White Westy Campmobile with the new style elevating roof and all the usual US spec options. This was to be the birth of Dylan. They returned a week later and committed themselves to putting their hearts and souls into a full restoration project down to the smallest details that would go on to last two years.

They thought hard about the design, wanting to create a bus that was smart yet subtle. In the end they opted for Sahara Beige paint, American Eagle rims, and a bespoke interior in 'Zebra', but as money was tight they had to make do with a reconditioned 1600 engine. The interior and exterior were Claire's domain—she relished the chance to choose everything from the colours inside and out, to »

46

VODKA IS
CHEAPER THAN
BOTOX
AND IT
PARALYSES
MORE MUSCLES

the interior layout, curtains, cushions and cab mats. And she certainly achieved a great finish throughout. The design of the interior was important as the layout had to be practical to suit the needs of a family with two children. To do this, a three-quarter rock and roll bed was fitted and a bespoke bed was made for the pop-top. The interior colour scheme took inspiration from the Sahara Beige exterior with matching tones on the upholstery, cushions and curtains.

Although completely rewarding in the end, the restoration was quite challenging and at times the couple felt like giving up. Along the way the family had to miss two planned holidays as the bus was just not ready on time. When Dylan was finally finished their first adventure was a 600-mile trip round Cornwall, and the bus behaved impeccably. Since then the family have been all over the UK to shows and on trips. Unfortunately, as is sometimes the case, some trips ended prematurely with Dylan on the back of a recovery truck, suffering one mechanical issue after another. But with the help of Dan and Claire's mechanic friend, Justin, all the issues were fixed and the bus is now running smoothly finally.

Future plans for the family are mainly to use and enjoy Dylan as much as possible, along with the ongoing upkeep of the engine as well as a fresh coat of paint applied. Though longer term plans

include a possible interior redesign. Owning Dylan has changed Dan and Claire's lives giving them the freedom to get away from it all. Regulars at their local Lowlife V-Dub Club events, they took a leap of faith and have gained many great experiences because of it. While there have been bad times—breaking down twice on the M69 on the way back from Dubdayz Summerfest on one of the hottest days of the year turning a one-hour trip into seven being a prime example—throughout the

Dylan is certainly a very much loved little camper and will continue to be used for many years to come. After all, he is part of the family!

year the family enjoy taking Dylan to shows and festivals and have even won a few trophies along the way. Dylan is certainly a very much loved little camper and will continue to be used for many years to come. After all, he is part of the family!●

DOUBLE
UP

Most pick-ups have led a hard
working life, so the chances of
finding one in mint condition,
especially a double cab, is the stuff
of barn find legend...

📷 : *David Eccles* 🎞 : *Simon Cooke*
Additional photographs courtesy: *Damian Van Spall*

aving seen the success of the Binz conversion, VW's own Doppelkabin model (often
abbreviated to Doka) was introduced in
1958—its ability to be both worker transport and
load-lugger added a new dimension to the VW
commercial range, which has continued across all
five generations ever since.

Built in November 1967, this Doka would have
been one of the first off the new T2 production
line. Finished in Light Grey with beige leatherette
interior, it was ordered by a banana plantation in
Gran Canaria, who specified a host of factory options to suit the hot and mountainous location, »

including the larger oil bath air cleaner, cab vent windows, additional dust sealing for the engine compartment, laminated windscreen, mountain ratio gearbox, as well as chrome hubcaps, steering lock, and tilt and bows.

Unlike many builder's pick-ups, this Doka led a relatively easy life on Gran Canaria just being used to transport bananas from the plantations to the packing sheds. Eventually making its way to

50

"I have always liked the shape of early Bay crew cabs. They seem so practical, being able to seat six (or five comfortably), and still have a heap of room in the back for all the kit." *Damian Van Spall*

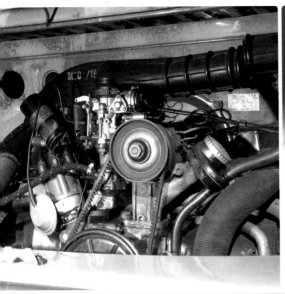

Tenerife, it was acquired a few years ago by Jaime Joseph Coello Vera of JJ Cars—the original classic VW garage on the island, serving the whole of the Canary Islands group. Still in sound condition, albeit with faded paintwork, all that was needed was new sliding windows, seals for the rear cab area and a thorough clean, before being stripped back and repainted in the original Light Grey.

Damian Van Spall had bought his first bus, a T3, back in 1992. It turned out to be a bit of a pig, so he replaced it with a 1974 Devon camper, which he still owns. "I have always liked the shape of early Bay crew cabs" Damian explained. "They seem so practical, being able to seat six (or five comfortably), and still have a heap of room in the back for all the kit." So when he saw the Doka advertised »

It was instantly clear the pictures didn't do the Doka justice—it would be hard to find one in such great condition. Jamie also turned out to be a mine of information about classic VWs

on TheSamba.com in 2011, he was very interested. Finding out it was in Tenerife, and with quite a high asking price, he did not pursue the matter; however something kept calling him. Then in September 2011 he booked a sailing holiday—from Spain down to the Canaries on a 100-year-old traditional wooden sailing boat. When he realised the trip finished in Tenerife he contacted the owner again to see if the Doka was still for sale; it was, so he arranged to view it upon arrival.

Reaching Tenerife in November, the van was waiting in the dock with Jamie for inspection. It was instantly clear the pictures didn't do the Doka justice—it would be hard to find one in such great condition. Jaime also turned out to be a mine of information about classic VWs, and on his return to England Damian decided to uncharacteristically throw caution to the wind. So a month later, he flew back to Tenerife, was collected by Jaime at the airport and taken by to his garage in Santa Cruz de Tenerife to finalise the deal over lunch!

Toying with the idea of driving the Doka back via Morocco and Spain, when Jaime explained that once the vehicle is registered as exported you risk getting it confiscated if you drive in Spain, Damian chose the less adventurous option of a shipping company to deliver it, which Jaime organised for him. He even threw in a high-ratio gearbox, as the low ratio option was not as effective on ordinary roads.

It arrived in Felixstowe where Damian collected it and drove it straight to Jim at IGS (Independent Garage Services) in Eastleigh for its first UK MoT. After a new set of RHD headlights and a full service, it had an MoT (on the chassis number). When the carburettor died a few weeks later IGS were luckily able to source an NOS one, maintaining the stock originality of the bus.

All in all, this simply has to be one of the cleanest and most original condition Bay Dokas you could come across—from the load bed through to the interior, everything is immaculate! ●

DELUXE
CAMPING

Looking resplendent in Chianti Red and Cloud White, this 1971 sunroof Deluxe Microbus has opened the doors to plenty of family-friendly fun for its new owners

📷 : *Graham Snodden* 🎞 : *David Eccles*

Built in June 1971 and featuring the newly introduced disc braking system, it was originally a seven-seater Deluxe Microbus featuring the factory steel sunroof and chrome trim as standard. Finished in Sierra Yellow under Pastel White it also carried the usual US-spec options of bumpers with over-riders, all red rear lenses, and front and rear side reflectors, as well as laminated windscreen, padded dash, and sealed beam headlights. First sold in Chicago, the bus eventually found its way to California where it gathered sand and a sun-baked appearance from years of

disuse. It had been imported to the UK and put up for sale as an MoT'd 'project' when Graham Snodden spotted it—attracted by the steel sunroof and the chance to create an interior for family use, he snapped it up. Upon delivery Graham fitted a new Bosch starter motor to fix some issues, but he knew that the interior and bodywork were best entrusted to professionals. Graham's basic philosophy was to make the bus useable in a way that kept the original features where possible, to add a level of reliability and comfort, but also bring things right up-to-date.

The bus was booked into Midland Paintwerks »

for a full respray in Chianti Red and Cloud White to stay with the 1971 year-correct VW scheme. Stuart and Drew set to work stripping the bus revealing what lurked under the paint—luckily only the cab floor and battery tray needed replacing, however many hours were then spent going back to bare metal and sealing with epoxy primer so that the many dents could be pulled out. The next step was to heat shrink some of the panels that had been stretched in previous accidents to add strength and ensure a good fit. This was followed by several coats of primer, followed by many coats of paint before it was ready for polishing and re-assembly.

The interior was mainly designed by Graham's wife, Lydia. Working with Scott at SJH Joinery she opted for a classic American Oak wooden camping interior, a three-quarter rock 'n' roll bed, Smev sink/hob combo and a Dometic fridge. As they wanted to colour-match some of the interior, scratch resistant Formica was sourced in Cloud White for the door panels and drawer fronts. For storage and flexibility, a removable, upholstered buddy seat sits in front of the load door side cabinet, where the TV/DVD is sited (on a spring loaded

TV lifter to hide it when not in use). A central unit across the gangway provides a really large, deep drawer, two smaller cupboards, and a solid oak cupholder for the front seat occupants. A unique bespoke touch that brings VW heritage to the interior is the fridge vent, created in the style of an Early Bay front grill. The interior table is stored under the overhead locker and can be used inside or outside with a Fiamma tripod. A 240v hook-up system, leisure battery/inverter and Webasto petrol-powered heater are fitted to complete the camping set-up, while the interior lighting was converted to

While the intention was never to build a show bus, this project developed a life of its own, and has won several trophies on its travels

LEDs to keep power consumption to a minimum.

The seats, door trims and headlining were colour-matched to the exterior and re-covered by Bromsgrove Auto Trimmers, as was the red upholstery and trim, with white piping and stitching providing finishing detail. Contrast is created by Steel Blue flooring and custom shiny parts—many sourced from USA—such as window winders, door handles, Gene Berg shifter and wood rim steering wheel. The 1600 TP engine features SP heads, Twin ICT 34s, Vintage Speed stainless exhaust, Pertronix electronic ignition, Pertronix leads, Bosch alter-

nator conversion and Gene Berg pulley, detailed to match the colour scheme. A RED9 wishbone adjustable front suspension kit is fitted with Spax adjustable shocks, rack and pinion steering, and standard discs (replaced with new discs/callipers) to bring it all up to date. The ride height is adjustable and has been dropped four inches to give on-road stability without compromising usability. The rear uses adjustable spring plates balancing the height of the front and standard shocks. VW Heritage Fuchs add to the custom stance and style.

While the intention was never to build a show bus, this project developed a life of its own, and has won several trophies on its travels. But the best experience the family have enjoyed was spending Christmas day in Cornwall on Polzeath beach in the bus, drinking hot chocolate at the end of a perfect day after a bracing walk on the coast. Using your bus is what VW ownership is all about after all. ●

CUSTOM
CREATION

Finished in Beryl Green under Pearl White, this stunning 1970 custom camper features a host of period accessories and goodies

📷 : *Jon Robinson-Pratt* 📖 : *David Eccles*

Looking around a wet campsite from the (dis) comfort of his tent back in 2002 with envious eyes, Jon Robinson-Pratt decided that a VW camper was the way to go. Approaching a local VW restoration company to build a van from one of the many rotten buses in their yard, they ended up going for a 1970 Danbury. It was basically a rolling shell that had been badly restored and lowered with no engine or pop-top that needed new doors, all four arches replacing, lower rear quarters, sills, a new front panel, the offside side panel behind the driver's door and the front beam. Originally finished in Light Grey, it had had several

Approaching a local VW resto company to build a van from one of the many rotten buses in their yard, they ended up going for a 1970 Danbury

paint combinations in its time, including Peach all over, including bumpers, wheels and chrome! Eventually Jon settled on the unique combination of Beryl Green and Pastel White.

The six month planned restoration actually dragged on for two years but finally, in 2004, he had a shiny bus with a hole in the roof and no interior! Rather than source another pop-top, Jon opted instead for a Paris Beetles ragtop sunroof, letting in light with the bonus of sleeping under the stars! Although originally a Danbury conversion, a Dormobile interior was deemed more practical with no sink and cooker added to aid storage. Jon re-upholstered the seat covers himself and made matching curtains in striped deckchair style material, and the original Dormobile table has been covered with stickers and cuttings in an 'old school skate' theme and covered with a Perspex top—the sticker bombing continued across all interior surfaces as well as the engine lid. Up front you'll find a pair of Recaros from an Astra

GTE which are "a bit hideous but damn comfortable!" Custom touches include the Mountney wood rimmed 15-inch wheel with VW logo, a dash-mounted tacho to keep an eye on the revs, an Empi trigger shifter, and an original Santa Cruz Speed Wheel gear knob complementing the skate theme. Finally there is a plethora of switches to operate all the different lights, lamps, and the Dixie 'General Lee' air horn!

Jon was inspired by the Dean Bradley Gadget Bus on the cover of Camper & Commercial magazine issue 11 that he describes as "the coolest Early Bay I had ever seen, and I decided this was the final look I wanted to achieve!" This meant the bus was subjected to some serious accessorising with the many parts amassed whilst waiting for the finished build—the number of period accessories is eye popping, helping with the look but not the drive. In 2006 the original engine went so a recon

Jon was inspired by the Dean Bradley Gadget Bus on the cover of Camper & Commercial issue 11— "the coolest Early Bay I had ever seen; I decided this was the final look I wanted to achieve!"

stock 1600 twin port engine was fitted and mated to a Bluebird Customs 4 into 1 stainless Quiet Pack exhaust. The addition of electronic ignition and a few chrome dress-up parts along with pinstriped tinware and a smoke grenade coil add to the eclectic look of the bus. The wheels are 15x4.5 pressed steel South African Rostyles (sprintstars) with the correct original chrome centre caps. Experimenting with various suspension configurations and tyre combinations over the years, the bus now sports a Creative Engineering Weedeater beam on the front with Wagens West dropped spindles, KYB shocks and skinny tyres to get it down nice »

62

The six month planned restoration actually dragged on for two years but finally, in 2004, he had a shiny bus with a hole in the roof and no interior!

and low but still be usable. The front arches have been tubbed slightly while the rear rests on Slamwerks Adjustable springplates set to the '1 notch down' position and then lowered as far as possible. Fatter tyres and KYB Gas Adjust shocks finish it off, leaving it really low, but still usable.

A fan of vintage signwriting, when Jon started up his own photography business he saw an opportunity to incorporate some and also advertise his business. Having done some pinstriping already, he decided to have a go at the signwriting himself—using a huge piece of tracing paper he transferred his design onto the side panel and set about work using a small signwriter's brush. The faded vintage look was achieved by careful use of T-CUT and the end result looks totally authentic!

Jon modestly describes his bus as, "most certainly not a show winner, the panels aren't straight, the door shut lines aren't anything to write home about and there is rust re-appearing! It gets used and abused but it is a good honest and solid bus that does what I need it to. I grinned from ear to ear when I finally drove it home after the two-year wait and I still grin from ear to ear every time I drive it nearly ten years later!" ●

The Caravelle was the top of the range people carrier.

BIGGER & BOXIER, BUT STILL
AIR-COOLED

The T3, aka T25, Brick or Wedge: 1979–1990

🏛 : *David Eccles*

Surprisingly, VW archives reveal that plans for the third generation of Transporter date back to 1974, with even a prototype looking very similar to the final version. Limited production commenced in May 1979 with the press launch, ready for full production in August.

The new styling drew on contemporary automotive design—gone were curves and rounded edges, instead flat surfaces and chiselled edges were de rigueur. The biggest surprise was that VW opted to retain the air-cooled motor sited at the rear, though plans for diesel and water-cooled engines were well advanced. A longer wheelbase and wider body meant the carrying capacity was now increased to 5.7 cubic metres. The running gear up front featured double wishbones, coil springs, telescopic dampers, anti-roll bars and rack and pinion steering, with semi-trailing arms and telescopic dampers at the rear, giving a smoother and safer ride. As well as a bigger side access door, the rear tailgate was now one single door, no separate engine lid.

1982: The air-cooled end

The engine options initially available were 1600cc and two-litre air-cooled versions, but in 1981 a water-cooled 1600cc diesel option became available, followed in 1982 by the replacement of the air-cooled petrol engines with 1.9 and 2.1-litre water-cooled versions, commonly known as Wasser Boxers. In 1985 the diesel lump came with the TDi turbocharged option. An easy way to spot whether a T3 is air- or water-cooled is by looking at the front end—early air-cooled models have a single grill; the water-cooleds have a second grill below it.

1985: 4WD arrives

Work on a 4WD all-terrain Transporter had begun in the late '70s on a T2 base, and though several prototypes were produced, it would not be till the T3 that 4WD capability was introduced. In 1982 VW entered into an agreement with Steyr-Daimler-Puch in Austria to design and produce an off-road version of the T3, the result being the launch

The Tristar was a luxury double cab pick-up—a forerunner of the SUV.

A syncro takes on the Sahara desert.

65

of the syncro (spelled with a lower case s) in 1985. Featuring viscous coupling and diff locks, a modified gearbox, raised suspension (the syncro stands 60mm higher than standard models) and underbody protection plates, the syncro's off-roading abilities have become legendary. Despite this only 25,000 were built up till 1989, though production continued in Austria until 1992 after the introduction of the T4.

One interesting development was the introduction of the Tristar in 1988—a luxury syncro double cab with rectangular headlights, power steering, and bull and roll cage bars. Clearly a forerunner to the ubiquitous luxury SUVs so popular these days!

A touch of class

Introduced in September 1981, the Caravelle saw VW return to the luxury market. Describing the vehicle as "offering all the comfort of a luxury car" and "executive transport for seven people", it broke away from the utilitarian, commercial models with two-tone paint, frame style headrests, foldable armrests, velour upholstery and trim, rear wash/wipe, chrome bumpers with rubber trim, carpeting throughout, and items like a fitted radio and locking petrol cap! The GL model was the top end version, featuring contoured rear seating. In 1985 an even more luxurious version—the Carat—was introduced and the distinctive twin rectangular halogen headlights of this model were adopted for the GL, along with power steering.

T3 campers

The introduction of the T3 co-incided with a change in camping interiors, with more emphasis on luxury, kitchen fitments, and the use of modern laminates and pastel shades.

Westfalia's new T3 campers were introduced in

Gone were curves and rounded edges, instead flat surfaces and chiselled edges were de rigeur

1979 (now known as the Joker). Over time the Joker was offered in several variants and seating arrangements, with special editions such as the Club Joker and Sport Joker. By 1988 Westfalia focused on two base models, rebranded as the California and the Atlantic. In recognition of the MPV market and demand for a vehicle that could combine leisure use and people carrier mode, VW introduced the Multivan, aka The Weekender, with moulded plastic sidewalls, small folding table, removable single seats, and a full-width rear seat/pull out bed.

Old names like Devon and Danbury produced T3 models, Danbury ceased trading in the late '80s and Devon sold off its camper side in 1989, but a whole host of new names entered the VW camper market of which Autohomes, Leisuredrive, Bilbo's and Autosleeper are still going strong and converting VWs.

The T3 was replaced with the radically new T4 generation that featuring a front-mounted engine in 1990, though a limited run of Special Edition Bluestar and Redstar models were produced in 1991/2, which were snapped up by workers in the VW factory! Worldwide sales for its production life topped 1.7 million, which was much less than the previous two generations—the time was right for VW to go back to the drawing board! ●

T3 or T25?
Despite being the third generation and designated T3, in the UK the model is commonly referred to as the T25. There are more theories about why this is so than there are about Kennedy, but the one most often quoted was simply to differentiate the T3 from the Type 3 (fastback/square-back/notchback). Other theories point to the chassis numbers and parts numbering prefixed with 25.

66

OFF-ROAD
CAMPER

This 4WD syncro started life as a panel van, but it's now a fully fitted camper that combines family with and off-road adventure

📷 : *Gareth Evans* 🛏 : *David Eccles*

I t was at Vanfest 2006 that Roy Crone was bitten by the VW bug. Until that point he'd always seen campers as an unnecessary luxury beyond a tent. That is until he got a close look around a Westfalia Joker syncro... he was hooked! Research began with Roy looking at every website dealing with syncros, the history, parts, what to look out for when buying, repairs, maintenance and converting, which resulted in him deciding a 16-inch syncro with a 2.1-litre engine was the ideal base. A major benefit is the suspension which was increased from the 14-inch version along with the brakes. However, given that only 2,138 16-inch syncros were ever made, with none exported to the UK, »

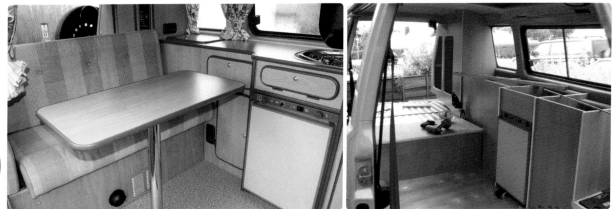

this version proved a little tricky to track down.

After some searching and consulting with CJ, ex-owner of Syncrospares, Roy set off in October 2006 for Belgium to see some of Mike's (aka Busman) stock, armed with a fistful of Euros. What he was met with was a stock 1989 LHD 16-inch syncro panel van with front and rear diff locks and a 2.1 DJ engine. Finished in orange, it had been exported to Sweden and had a basic DIY conversion by a previous owner—it was in sound condition despite being a working panel van and the engine had been rebuilt, so the deal was done!

Back in the UK after registration and an MoT, Roy got to work. First a new VC coupling had to be fitted before the strip out and clean up began. Roy decided to get the paint done before fitting anything, so the van went off for a respray in its original orange. Next the windows were put in before taking it to MCC Reimo in Manchester for the pop-top roof to be installed. Deciding the »

After some searching and consulting with CJ, ex-owner of Syncrospares, Roy set off in October 2006 for Belgium to see some of Mike's (aka Busman) stock, armed with a fistful of Euros

70

For the 25-year anniversary of the syncro—and after a gearbox rebuild by Aidan Talbot in Warrington—Roy enjoyed a trip over to an event in Mammut Park in Germany, and had great fun on the off-road courses

Westfalia layout was a good starting point, at the beginning of January 2007 once the bus was back, he emailed Mike at MPI Campers in North Wales and asked if he would let Roy do a full measured survey of his T3 Westfalia, which he kindly agreed to. Based on this, Roy started some scale drawings, but they very quickly began to change! J&S Upholstery were commissioned to re-upholster the seats both front and back—and they also supplied lightweight plywood and edge trims for the units, curtain rails, hooks, and lots of helpful advice.

After another trip back to Reimo in Manchester for hinges, door catches, table legs and again some tips from their fit-out guys, they ordered more interior fittings from CAK Tanks in Kenilworth, including lights, sink and twin-burner combi unit, tap, gas fittings and power points. The van already had a fridge and onboard water tank fitted which were able to be reused. Finally, all the bits amassed, Roy started the interior build. Meanwhile Roy's wife, Sara, set to work on the curtains,

upholstered panels, and painting the floor before installing the insulation, over boarding and finally the lino flooring. Lastly, the electrical work was carried out and by July 2007 the van was ready... just one day before their holiday in Cornwall. The bus performed superbly and camping, even in rain, was just bliss! A couple of days into the holiday, the gearstick sheared off—a temporary repair with a screwdriver as a gearstick lasted, before a replacement stick was couriered direct to their pitch by CJ.

Since finishing his bus, Roy has carried out a variety of maintenance jobs—including fitting stainless steel fuel tank straps, a rite of passage for any syncro owner—and fitted a number of accessories—an original pair VW van mirrors being of particular note.

For the 25-year anniversary of the syncro—and after a gearbox rebuild by Aidan Talbot in Warrington—Roy enjoyed a trip over to an event in Mammut Park in Germany. They had great fun on the off-road courses and meeting like-minded

owners. The van ran brilliantly until Roy was 80 miles from home when fourth gear sheared. Luckily, Roy could drop the box in the following week for Aidan to do a full rebuild, so the van was back on the road within a month. Designing and converting the bus himself around his family's needs, Roy has created a camper he can use and love. And with further trips through Europe planned, including travelling to Italy via the Alps, he is definitely going to get the most out of his camper. ●

HAVE CAMPER
WILL TRAVEL

Finding himself envious of a friend's 1979 T3 after going to shows in a car and caravan for years, Jeff Blunt finally decided to find one for himself

📷 : *Nicky Connor* 📷 : *Dave Richards*

A nd what a search it was. After three years of bus spotting at shows, Jeff knew what he wanted and happened to find it somewhat by chance when he stopped off at Bustypes enroute to viewing another bus. Wandering the trade area, sat on an auto-traders pitch, surrounded by the usual air cooled bits and pieces, was a T3 only just brought back from Stuttgart whose owner had put up a 'testing the waters' for sale sign. Jeff paid there and then and was a happy man for it—it was every bit as good as he'd thought, with the original Westfalia interior all there and in excellent condition. The body was also sound and although the Masala Red paint was faded almost to pink, there was no trace of corrosion in the seams, under the wheel arches, anywhere. »

JFY 362

74

It came on 17-inch Porsche Boxter S wheels—Jeff hated them, but stuck with them until he found his choice of replacement; a set of OZ Futura forged three-piece split rims, which are big! They are 9x18 at the front shod in 225/40, and an almost unbelievable 11x18 and 275/35 at the back. Measuring and remeasuring to find out exactly what he could get away with, he had the wheels built to his specifications. As they are relatively heavy with the tyres fitted, he converted the hubs to wheel studs to make mounting them easier. And as wheels this size don't really just bolt on, to make them work properly, the suspension was also amended. It was lowered by 50mm using shorter springs at the front and airbags at the rear; the trailing arms were stripped and powdercoated. Shorter shock absorbers were fitted, it was re-bushed all round and a camber correction kit was fitted to the back. This eliminates all this negative camber, wheels at tragic, tyre shredding angles malarky, and makes it ride and handle properly. Lastly, Jeff fitted stainless, braided brake lines, some additional interior lighting, a few billet aluminium interior goodies, and it was ready to go.

Jeff and his wife have covered some serious mileage in their T3. From their base in the West Midlands, they regularly holiday in Devon and Cornwall. He took it north to the highlands of Scotland, and south into Europe, down to Cap Cerbére on

the Spanish border and all around France where the 1.6-litre straight four diesel engine covered over 3,500 miles in a fortnight. All at around 450 miles to a tank of fuel and without a sign of distress or over-heating. The campervan has also done many VW shows—it won a trophy at the first VDub Island in 2011, while at Busfest the Reimo Cate rear motorbike rack that fits a T3 was a real one of a kind find that means Jeff's Vespa GTS 300 scooter can now travel with them too.

Jeff then had the camper repainted with help from a workmate just before he left the company. The faded red and pink paint was flatted back to reveal even less in the way of corrosion than had been expected. It was primed, a few layers of base coat and finally clear lacquered. Disaster. As they set about refitting door handles and the like, it was apparent that something was not quite right. It looked like the paint wasn't quite dry, but it was. And as time went on, it got worse... even flies crashing into the front when driving along damaged the finish. Further investigation revealed that although the lacquer was fine, the base coat colour had remained soft. There was no

Jeff and his wife have covered some serious mileage in their T3. From their base in the West Midlands, they regularly holiday in Devon and Cornwall. He took it north to the highlands of Scotland, and south into Europe, down to Cap Cerbere on the Spanish border and all around France

option. Jeff was forced to take the bull by the horns and strip off all of the new paint, this time right back to bare metal. Everything was stripped, everything removed, interior, windows, the lot. Every last drop of paint came off using paint stripper and heat guns. It took him 12 weeks working weekends and evenings. And then it was repainted properly by another of Jeff's workmates, Rob, who knew what he was doing and the result is spectacular!

With everything refitted and finished, Jeff has been driving and using his camper ever since—it even returned to winning ways with another trophy on its travels to Camper Jam. But more importantly, it's a proper campervan that's used how it's supposed to be. ●

AROUND THE
WORLD

Filmmaker For A Cause (FMFAC), a small non-profit volunteer organisation, find the perfect vehicle to hit the road on a year-long global tour

 : Stuart Thomas 🖪 : Dave Richards

With the cost of flights, car rentals, hotels, etc. being prohibitive, the project had been abandoned until the idea hatched of buying a bus. After buying a Bay window on eBay, Randall Brown from FMFAC realised it was a little too small and in "horrible shape" to be up to the task at hand. So instead, Randall decided to buy a 'cheap' syncro and fix it up, then volunteer it to FMFAC for a year for the project. Easy he thought. Well, it's easy if all you want to do with your syncro is potter down to the shops in a dusting of British snow. But if you want to live in it for a year whilst driving it around the world it can be a little bit tricky, and more importantly, certain components need upgrading or specialist items added. And with this bus it is very much a case of form following function.

The syncro he purchased came already fitted with a 2.2-litre Subaru engine, but without the exact details of what had been done to the engine and needing to trust that it wouldn't fail during any part of the tour where access to garages would be limited, he decided to fit a new set-up. He decided on a Bostig two-litre Ford Zetec installation. "We wanted a simple conversion, worldwide parts availability, full documentation of the system, and of course, reliability." The biggest thing for Randall was that every nut and bolt and the wiring

79

diagram is detailed in the Bostig manual, so if it couldn't be fixed by themselves, they could pass the book to someone who could.

After the engine, the suspension, wheels and tyres were one of the hardest systems to finalise, and one of the most important. With the addition of skid plating, full expedition gear, and a chest full of spares, he would be carrying a lot of weight. Coupled with the need to handle rough roads for thousands of miles, this was a big decision. Powdercoated black steel wheels were an easy choice—steel is more forgiving and can always be hammered straight. For tyres, proven BF Goodrich AT/KOs were chosen. The suspension

> After the engine, the suspension, wheels and tyres were one of the hardest systems to finalise, and one of the most important

was upgraded to use Burley Motorsports custom 16-inch rear trailing arms and Burley's front tubular upper control arms, which all pivot on precision machined urethane bushings. After lots of research, they found GMB coilovers who had provided the set-up on a similar expedition bus, whose shocks and springs would be able to handle the weight, provide excellent on and off-road handling, and give a comfortable ride. Finally »

To tackle sound and thermal insulation the team opted on a hybrid approach, coating the complete interior with Noxudol—a spray-on sound deadener with anti-rust properties—along with a closed cell foam insulation sourced from a hot rod company which does the job perfectly

they had the front differential and transmission rebuilt, and also added a locking front differential with a viscous coupling instead of a solid shaft.

To tackle sound and thermal insulation the team opted on a hybrid approach, coating the complete interior with Noxudol—a spray-on sound deadener with anti-rust properties—along with a closed cell foam insulation sourced from a hot rod company which does the job perfectly. That left the windows—the largest source of heat gain and loss—upon which they fitted a full curtain set from SewFine and Limo-tinted all the side windows. The rear hatch and front side windows are a slightly lighter level, to comply with legislation. They have camped in temps as low as -2°C with the top popped, without heat, and they were comfortable with just a blanket. Job done!

Starting as a tin-top bus, the interior was built from scratch with a custom interior shipped flat-packed from Europe. Where possible they've utilised space to house tanks and appliances, and had custom boxes made to fit cabinets to make it easier to empty the bus for certain border crossings. All the interior panels are by SewFine and everything is finished in black! There was concern about using dark colours with the heat levels they'd face, but with the tinted windows this hasn't been an issue and helps the camper look clean.

Finally, in terms of accessories found on the bus, all the stuff that makes the trip and filming on location workable, including: the massive, extra 13.5-gallon fuel tank; a huge array of lithium

batteries required to keep all the filming gear charged; a 1,000W inverter; a VSM system used to monitor the electrics; a solar panel on the roof and one that opens out with the awning; an Eberspacher providing heat; a 13-gallon tank for water; there's a winch to get out of tight spots; and even a compressor to power air tools! This is a very, very different type of bus, but one that does its job perfectly in one of few vehicles up to the challenge. ●

SCOOBY
SINGLE CAB

With its matt black paint, two-litre Subaru lump and a whole host of modifications, this T3 single cab is hard as nails, and very, very fast!

📷 : Simon Cooke 🎙 : David Eccles

When Finlay Paton was looking for something cheap that could haul bikes and fencing back in 2009, he stumbled upon a tatty T3 pick-up with no tax or MoT, and at £650 he couldn't walk away! Built in 1990 with a 1.9 DX petrol motor it had been abused, but had lots of potential.

After lowering it by 80mm all round, an engine conversion was next on the cards after the old 1.9 wasserboxer blew a coolant hose and he had to limp home from London. He already had the engine—a Subaru 2.0 EJ20 Turbo—so set about converting the pick-up into a Scooby single cab. As some body modifications were required due to the dreaded tinworm, he stripped the bus and took it to a friend's body shop, Zealou5 (fast road Nissan Skyline specialists), who replaced the floor, all four wings, rear panels, front scuttle, front and rear screen surrounds, the back of the cab, and the loadbed floor. New rear wings with a wider stance were fabricated and fitted, along with newly fabricated sills »

"It's fast as hell and great for carrying bikes, fence panels or anything at all. Plus I get more looks in my old T3 than in my new T5 Sportline." *Fin Paton*

and engine scoops at the back for better cooling before repainting in Satin Black Rustolium finish. To provide contrast detail, the roof was painted in Peugeot Ermine White, with the bumpers and certain parts powdercoated and finished in Cream.

The wheels, Mercedes CLK 17x7J on the front and 16-inch steels banded to ten inches on the rear (also Cream), have been fitted with Acellera 205/50/17 and Kumaho 225/50/16 tyres, and have been finished with a glow-in-the-dark powdercoat. Other off-the-wall custom touches can be seen in the Stella Artois beer can centre caps, the polished, drilled door handles, and the bike sprocket surround for the front badge.

Mechanically the brakes have been uprated with black diamond discs, pads and Goodrich braided lines, and new CV joints were fitted. In order to provide good access to the engine, the new flooring on the rear deck has been made fully removable. Fin then set about fitting the Subaru lump using a full RJES conversion kit and a TSR loom. This also involved using handmade 2.5-inch downpipe and the fabrication of a full exhaust system from mild steel. This has been replaced with new stainless headers and full stainless three-inch downpipe from Janspeed, along with a single silencer box, so now it sounds much more Scooby. Other mods include a rebuilt gearbox from Aiden Talbot, a syncro locking diff, and a charge cooler in place of the intercooler, later upgraded with a Pejero intercooler fan to aid air flow.

With the engine producing 248bhp, Fin's first track day trip shocked a few people. Even though it kept spinning a rear wheel under full load, he had to carry 50 litres of water to keep the back end down! And to emphasise its drag styling and inspiration, he added twin parachute 'brakes' at the back to really set the tone. Other external features and acces-

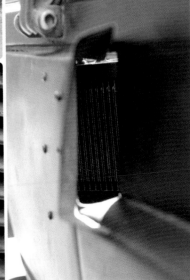

sories include a Thule roof spoiler for high speed stability, smoked front indicator lenses, and a spotlight mounted on the cab roof rear. The Rose badging and graphics refer to the Rose Versand brand—a reputable German company that has specialised in bikes and biking accessories since 1907—representing Fin's other passion.

The cab itself still sports the original dash and gauges, with the addition of a dash-mounted rev counter. Extra sound-proofing has been added to the cab floor and doors, and a Retro Sounds stereo is linked to 6x9 speakers mounted in a custom housing behind the seats. A pair of Sparco race seats with Schroth harnesses and custom-made harness bar devlop the drag theme, while an extended carbon handbrake, furry dice and 8-ball gearknob add finishing detail. A smattering of stickerbombing on the rear wall completes the look.

As with many buses, this one is still a work in progress according to Fin. Future plans include having the rear deck rebuilt in metal, relocating the charge cooling rad up front, a stiffer anti-roll bar up front and an additional rear version, and to lift the front end by 10mm to even out wheel loading. A new roof spoiler, vintage steering wheel and mock wheelie bar are also on the list! For now, however, Fin's VW obsession and need for speed continues to be satiated by using his excellently stylised and engineered T3 pick-up.

"It's fast as hell and great for carrying bikes, fence panels or anything at all. Plus I get more looks in my old T3 than in my new T5 Sportline, and though I must admit I still miss my old Golf Rallye, the pick-up is a blast to drive—in every sense of the word!" ●

BIG
WINDOW
BOY

With production of T3s continuing in South Africa until 2002, this restyled 'big window' model was first introduced in 1991 featuring—you guessed it—larger side windows...

📷 : *Fleur and Kevin Challis* 📷 : *David Eccles*

The new 'facelift' VWSA model was available from early 1991. The side windows (which were opening sliders) now extended down to where the body bezel was, with another unique difference to previous T3s being the inclusion of rear-facing vents in the air scoop at the rear. Balancing the look, a black bezel under the front windscreen gave the illusion of a larger screen,

while a South Africa-only design front grill arrangement, twin circular headlights (rectangular for Caravelles), a brush guard under the grill, and a full-width lower grill which incorporated the indicators. There was also a slightly different dashboard design inside, but perhaps the most significant change was the introduction of the VW Audi five-cylinder, fuel-injected engine, available in 2.3, 2.5 and 2.6 versions. This offered more power and torque than the six-cylinder versions, combined with the fuel »

88

This bus was among the first built, and was delivered in February 1992 to its owner who traded in a BMW 325i as half the purchase price! It was a top of the range Caravelle Carat model

economy and pep of four-cylinder engines, which, when mated to a five-speed box, made for a much improved driving experience more akin to a car than a van. Larger, vented front discs were also fitted to cope with the increase in performance.

This bus was among the first built, and was delivered in February 1992 to its owner who traded in a BMW 325i as half the purchase price! It was a

top of the range Caravelle Carat model, so featured all the model features such as power steering, central locking, alloy wheels, metallic paint, GRP bumpers, front spoiler, window protection bars, rear wash/wipe, and 30mm lowering springs, as well as luxury velour trim and full carpeting. For multi-purpose use, the rear seat laid down to form a bed, while the middle row of seats consisting of a two-person bench with a third seat that could either fold sideways for improved access or flip over to form a small table with cup holders. Finished in a SA metallic silver-blue, it was originally fitted with a front protection bar option (now removed) and towbar.

Exported to the UK in April '94, it was registered in June and benefitted from comprehensive records showing it had its last service in South Africa on the 24/02/94 with 44,749km on the clock and the first recorded service in the UK was on the 05/06/95 with 59,052 km by AFG in Solihull. By 2001 the bus had had three owners and went on sale again, just when John Alflatt had started a search for a bus to use as both a camper and load lugger. As he had worked in South Africa and driven the five-cylinder big window buses, John knew that they are lovely to drive with a very modern feel. So he didn't hesitate, when he spotted one for sale in the UK he had to have it!

Generally, the bus was still in good condition, albeit needing some bodywork repairs to the sliding door and rear wheel arch, as well as a new clutch. The distinctive metallic blue paint was initially tricky to match, but the team at Resto Classics in Hastings, who carried out the work, found that 86G Metallic Blue blended in perfectly. And as John describes: "It hasn't been so much a restoration as gradual planned maintenance. A lot of parts have been replaced, repaired or upgraded, but visually, I like the very clean simple look, so nothing major has been altered. However, over the years it has had a multitude of parts replaced from the digital clock to the fuel tank!" »

With no plans to change anything—even though John is an admirer of bespoke interiors—and in keeping with the 'keep it stock' plan, the only addition to the bus has been a dual battery system under the swivelling passenger seat. He finds the versatility of the Carat interior ideal for his needs, and describes the bus as "the perfect all-round vehicle!" He continues, "It fits a standard parking bay and most parking lots; you can move house or make it your house; carry surfboards or floorboards; and be the envy of everybody without any depreciation! And I still think it's fun when other VW drivers wave or walk over for a chat. Every journey seems like an adventure and I never tire of seeing the distinctive shape patiently waiting for me on my return from the waves, mountains or shops!" ●

TALKIN' 'BOUT YOUR GENERATION!

SO, YOU WANT TO
BUY A BUS

David Eccles tackles the tricky topic of classic bus buying. So just what should you be considering when buying a vintage vehicle?

📷 : *Various* 🖚 : *David Eccles*

Which Generation is for you?

There's no doubt the Split, with its iconic looks and classic lines wins the cuteness appeal. But remember you are looking at something that's 45-plus years old, which can be costly to maintain and hideously expensive to buy! And unless a more powerful engine has been installed it will also be slow—but that's part of the fun!

A Bay window bus still has the charm and appeal, with the pre-1972 versions (Early Bays) especially sought after. The T3 (T25) on the other hand may lack the charisma of Splits and Bays, but drives like a modern vehicle still, and things like power steering can be found.

Are you looking for something that is a blank canvas to put your stamp upon, or do you want something that's all been done up and restored? In the end it probably comes down to budget—how much are you willing to spend to get the bus of your dreams?! »

94

95

Finding the right bus

Do a bit of research, go to shows and events to look at models and talk to owners, decide what works best for the lifestyle you want and the budget available. Having decided what generation of bus you are looking for, the best place to turn to next is the for sale pages on the major club forums (see box out); it is here you find a community that offers advice and support and where you can often find a bus that has clearly been loved and cared for. Another good internet site is TheSamba.com, which although predominantly US-based, does have buses for sale in Europe and the UK. (I sold my Split via the SSVC site, and an Early Bay through TheSamba.com, both in just a few days!)

Most VW shows have a for sale area—the biggest being Bus Freeze, Stanford Hall and Busfest, where you can wander round and really have a good look at a range of things.

There are also many excellent enthusiast-run businesses that offer buses for sale, including projects they can restore to your budget and taste.

And, of course, there is the dreaded eBay... all I will say on this is caveat emptor (buyer beware). Buying blind or from pics and seller's words alone may turn up a gem, but may also turn up a rotbox!

Importing

With old buses commanding premium prices and continuing high demand, large numbers are now imported to the UK, mainly from the USA. Buses that have lived in a dry, warm climate are often still quite solid and rust-free, only needing tidying rather than fully restoring. Buses coming from South Africa and Australia will also be RHD mod-

> DO A BIT OF RESEARCH, GO TO SHOWS AND EVENTS TO LOOK AT MODELS AND TALK TO OWNERS, DECIDE WHAT WORKS BEST FOR THE LIFESTYLE YOU WANT AND THE BUDGET AVAILABLE

els! Importing a private sale is straightforward, with many companies geared up to handling all the arrangements.

What should I look out for?

It's not in the scope of this overview to give a detailed account of what sorts of things to check out when you view a bus, but try to get the owner talking... which will not be a problem for an enthusiast. How long have they owned it? What kind of work has been done on the bus? Why are they selling it? What can they tell you about its history?

Rust is the biggest problem on an old bus. Rust in the chassis rails, structural points such as outriggers, jacking points, roofs and gutter sections, should be treated with extreme caution. Cab floors, battery trays and outer sills are fairly common rust areas on buses, even from 'dry' locations, and are fairly easily fixed, but corrosion beyond such limits will need extensive work. If a bus has been repaired and/or repainted, ask if there are »

TAKE IT FOR A DRIVE—HOW DOES IT FEEL? DOES IT PULL THROUGH THE GEARS SMOOTHLY? TURN IN A TIGHT CIRCLE AND LISTEN FOR KNOCKS. HOW DO THE BRAKES FEEL?

photos of work being done. If it has been lowered or modified ask who has done the work, and with lowering, how it has been done.

Look at window surrounds, lift cab floor mats, use a magnet to check for filler repairs. Listen to the engine tick over when it has warmed up, check for fluid and oil leaks, is the engine bay clean? Check all lights, wipers, etc, work.

Take it for a drive—how does it feel? Does it pull through the gears smoothly? Turn in a tight circle and listen for knocks. How do the brakes feel?

With any camper interior, check the condition of the units and cabinets and if equipment works. If you are looking at a period, mainly original interior, is everything there? Missing items may be hard to source or very expensive! Whilst the blank canvas of an empty Microbus or Kombi may be exactly what you want to create your own interior, remember bespoke fitted interiors are not cheap and many companies are booked up for a year in advance.

Be patient

Remember the old adage "don't buy the first bus you see"—buying a camper is an emotional investment and it's easy to fall in love at first sight! Many people spend six months looking for their perfect bus and often a bus turns out not to be quite as described or pictured when go to you see it. You have to kiss a lot of frogs till you find your Prince (or Princess), but with patience you will find the right bus for you.

PRICE GUIDE

The figures suggested opposite are based on prices asked and paid in 2013. These are guidelines only and should not be taken as definitive. Prices have spiralled in the past few years and there seems to be no end in sight to that trend. Prices also tend to fluctuate according to season.

Please note: We have used five broad categories to group buses by price band. ●

97

Project bus
Typically part finished, or an empty shell with no engine, or an import in need of restoration

Usable bus
On the road but needing some attention to maintain or keep/make roadworthy

Part restored bus
Something tidy, fairly original and stock, and mechanically sound, with either original interior or a more modern makeover

Restored, complete bus
Including a full restoration or an original paint/condition bus that's been protected or modified, or something with an original camping interior

Fully restored/fully original mint condition
Potential show or Concours D'elegance winner!

Split bus 1950–1967
Unless you are a real enthusiast with deep pockets, forget pre-1955 Barndoor buses! The Deluxe Microbus (Samba) commands prices way higher than guidelines below.
Project bus
£5,000–£7,000
Usable bus
£7,000–£10,000
Part restored bus
£10,000–£18,000
Restored, complete bus
£19,000–£30,000
Fully restored/fully original mint condition
£35,000–£100,000!

Bay window bus 1967–1979
Westfalia campers in original condition are highly sought after models.
Project bus
£2,500–£4,500
Usable bus
£5,000–£8,000
Part restored bus
£9,000–£14,000
Restored, complete bus
£15,000–£19,000
Fully restored/fully original mint condition
£20,000–£30,000

T3 1979–1990
Caravelles and syncro models are the most expensive T3s.
Project bus
£800–£2,000
Usable bus
£2,500–£5000
Nice clean Multivan/Caravelle/day van
£3,500–£6,500
Restored, complete bus
£7,000–£10,000
Fully restored/fully original mint condition
£10,000–£19,000

Custom wheels, stance, paint and pinstriping turn even a humble panel van into a stunner.

THE ENGINE IS
IN THE FRONT!

T4: 1990–2003

☎ : David Eccles

Production of the T4 actually started in January 1990, but it did not go on public sale until August. Recognising a changing market and consumer needs, and taking advantage of modern automotive technology, VW threw out the old rear-engined layout, opting instead to place the engine and drive up front. This came as an unwelcome shock to many enthusiasts and lovers of the iconic box on wheels! The driver cabin was further back and the carrying space had to be slightly decreased to 5.4 cubic metres, though a new long wheelbase version could carry 6.3 cubic metres. Also new was the cab plus chassis only option, much welcomed by coachbuilders. Access at the rear was twin opening doors for commercial vehicles and via an opening tailgate for leisure models.

Five new-engine front-mounted transverse engine options were introduced: a 1.9 or 2.4 litre diesel; and 1.8, 2 and 2.5-litre petrol versions.

The new T4 found instant commercial success with businesses and fleet operators, and commercial versions—especially panel vans—easily outsold any other model.

A New Look

In 1996, recognising the need to separate the commercial and leisure markets—and to make way for the new VR6 en-

Westfalia's Joker models were replaced with the rebranded California in 1998.

gine option—the Caravelle and Mulitivan models received a front end makeover to give more of a luxury 'passenger car' look. Featuring a new dash, an extended bonnet and redesigned headlamp clusters and grills, these models are often known as 'long nose' T4s. The restyle was subsequently offered on other models and such was the impact on appearance, that many people now choose to have a 'long nose' conversion carried out on former commercials that are being transformed into bespoke campers. 1996 also saw the introduction of the 2.5TDI engine, deemed by enthusiasts as the T4's best in terms of performance, economy and reliability.

T4 campers

Westfalia, as VWs chosen partner, was still the most popular and biggest seller. The new T4 campers were marketed as the California, and the interior was very much influenced by the T3 California and Atlantic conversions. High roof versions were also available including a top end mini-motorhome model named the Exclusive. Many badged Special Editions were also produced, such as the Event, the Beach and the Blue.

Most Westfalia models were LHD, however, so UK conversions by Holdsworth, Autosleeper, Bilbo and Reimo were popular here. Although

The new T4 found instant commercial success with businesses and fleet operators

small firms such as Calypso Campers (also still going strong) began to offer one-off bespoke builds, where a customer would not only choose fabrics, colours and fittings, but they were also involved in tailoring the design and layout to their own tastes and needs. Partly fuelled by the insatiable demand for VW campers, the rising cost of 'classics', the lack of a huge pool of second hand campers, and the demand for something that is more personal and individual, there began the move to bespoke conversions offering a personal and original service. Buying a new or used ex-commercial (the ubiquitous white builder's van usually) and having it converted to your own tastes was not only more affordable, it also meant you had something unique!

A walk round any VW show nowadays reveals the T4 has been reclaimed by a new generation of owners keen to modify, customise and create a personal style.

With a worldwide sales figure of 1.9 million, the T4, with the engine in the front, proved to be an unqualified success, one ready to be built on with the advent of the new T5. ●

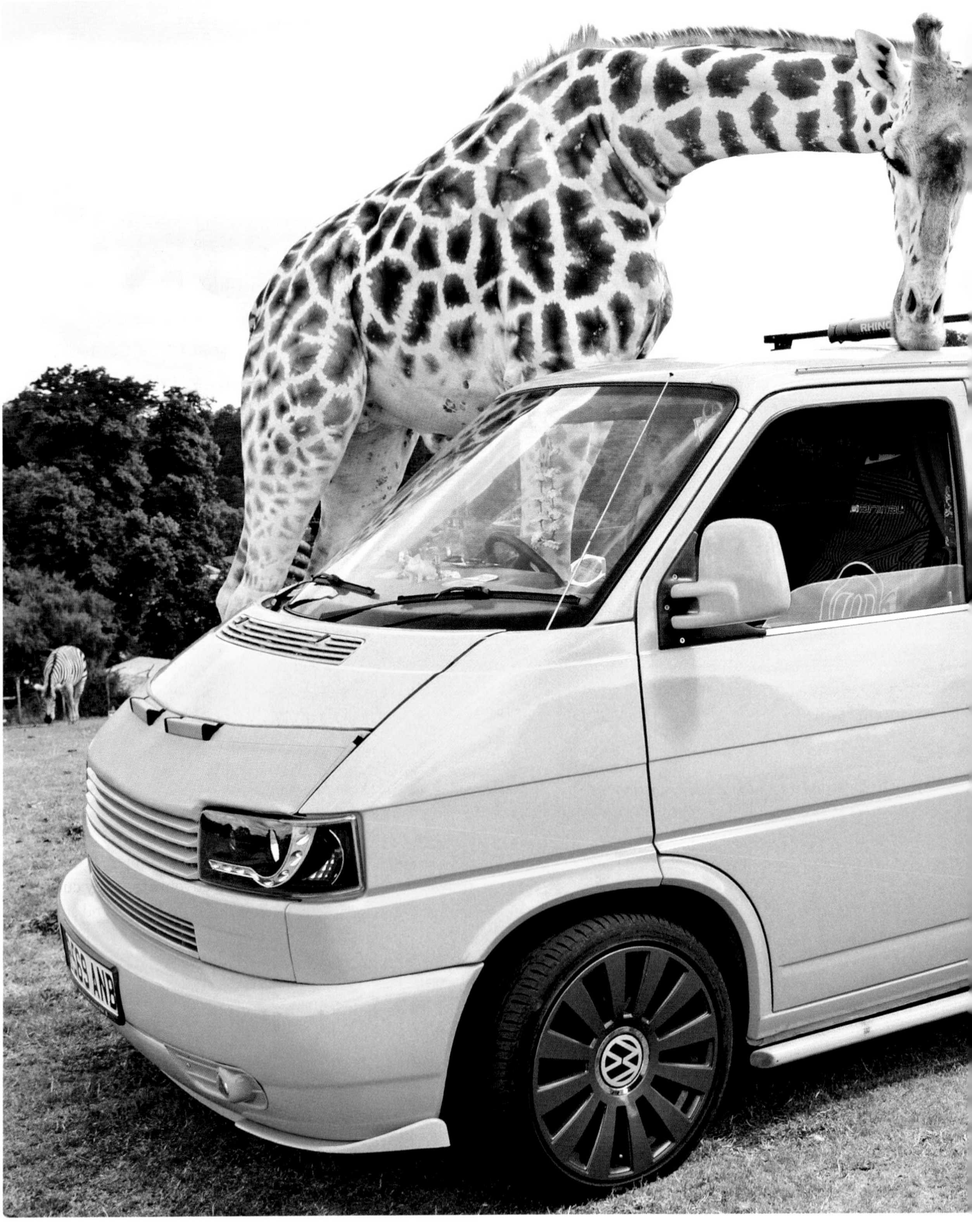
RHINO

SAFARI AND
SURF

He may be a first time convertor, but adding his carpentry skills to an excellent concept and love of the VW lifestyle, has resulted in something fantastic!

📷: *Nicky Connor* 🖊: *Alan Hayward*

S am Taylor's story is a familiar one. As a child he loved family camping holidays as they meant fun, freedom and adventure. They cultivated a love of the outdoor lifestyle, biking and surfing in particular, and Sam couldn't wait to have a van of his own to enable his outdoor pursuits. He saved up and bought his first van at only 19, an empty work van which had a few scars but seemed a solid base.

Sam was working as a carpenter and joiner for a pine furniture manufacturer at the time, so had all the relevant skills and access to the raw materials for a conversion. Along with a general tidy up and mechanical overhaul, he built the basic camper he wanted and set off on his weekend adventures, surfing at Woolacombe and the like, in his trusty 70-odd horsepower, newly converted T4 camper. »

102

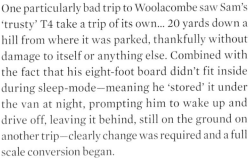

One particularly bad trip to Woolacombe saw Sam's 'trusty' T4 take a trip of its own... 20 yards down a hill from where it was parked, thankfully without damage to itself or anything else. Combined with the fact that his eight-foot board didn't fit inside during sleep-mode—meaning he 'stored' it under the van at night, prompting him to wake up and drive off, leaving it behind, still on the ground on another trip—clearly change was required and a full scale conversion began.

Together with his friend, Steve Fletcher, they hatched a plan. Steve runs Auto Revival, a paint and body shop in Droitwich; initially Sam asked for a duck egg blue and was shocked when he was handed box containing about 1,500 different blues! The shade was chosen, and although Sam admits it turned out different to what he'd expected, he loves it. Turning to the inside, Sam did the work himself following an obvious beach theme, with a beach-comber driftwood vibe coming through loud and

Together with his friend, Steve Fletcher, they hatched a plan. Steve runs Auto Revival, a paint and body shop in Droitwich

clear. Basing the concept around the need to carry an eight-foot board and with no need for carrying passengers in the rear, he came up with an unusual solution—a side facing bed/seat was constructed, under which you'll find copious storage for camping paraphernalia like chairs, a canopy awning, plus the obligatory flag and flagpole. Sadie, Sam's partner requested an easy-to-access full-length wardrobe, which can be found behind the bed. Opposite is a double cupboard, one side of which houses all the important stuff like leisure battery, gas bottle, etc., with the other side being utilised for food. Above this cupboard is a useful storage shelf, and set in the roof an unusual LED light set-up. »

By no means did Sam restrict his imagination and carpentry skills to the bus interior. No, the astute will have noticed some innovative wooden sidebars—they are none other than a pair of pine handrails

Behind the front passenger seat is a truly unique curved cupboard. The reason for the curve is to allow room for Sam's all-important seven-foot-ten Mini Mal board to be stored indoors when the van is in sleep-mode. In the base of the curved cupboard are a sub box and an amp, while the top bit—accessed by the gas ram activated lid—houses a campervan equivalent of the 'Man Drawer', which contains everything from zip ties and a lighter, to board wax and some spanners for board and bus maintenance. An excellent use of space and foresight.

By no means did Sam restrict his imagination and carpentry skills to the bus interior. No, the astute will have noticed some innovative wooden sidebars—they are none other than a pair of pine handrails, cut to shape and size then varnished to within an inch of their lives to bring the wooden beach theme to the forefront of the excellent exterior too. You will also have noticed the Dream Catcher Camper logo—an idea that Steve and Sam have floated, and another string to SGT (Sam's carpentry business) and Auto Revival's bow that they plan to expand upon in the future. A final word on SGT, Sam does quite a bit of contract work, and when discussing the potential location for the upcoming photo shoot with a Split-screen van-owning customer, he chimed in with "I may be able to help you there!" Sam's customer works at the West Midlands Safari Park in Kidderminster and very generously allowed photographer, Nicky Connor, and Sam unrivalled access for some amazing shots.

So the story ends with Sam owning a stunning—and Camper Jam award-winning van. But most importantly, owning the van that young Sam has always dreamed of owning... and all this by the grand old age of 22. ●

THE ULTIMATE CAT VAN

Every now and then a bus comes along that is beyond unique. Sometimes that works and sometimes it doesn't, but the 'Dogapillar' pulls off unique perfectly

📷 : *Grant Richards* 🏍 : *Alan Hayward*

Starting life as a 2000 vintage T4 LWB Doka, with a dropside tipper body out back and 88bhp 2.5 Tdi up front, this pick-up was scruffy and a bit battered when it arrived with new owner, Bernard Woods. But it was perfect for Bernard, who wanted a base on which to create something unique and something that would be talked about. The 'Dogapillar' certainly ticks the boxes.

Starting work, the first job was to remove the tipper body so expert aluminium fabricator and friend, Ade Tilly of Stainless Till Exhausts, could set about constructing a new rear deck to sit directly upon the revealed ladder chassis. Covered in checker-plate, Ade's neat construction welds enhance the industrial look Bernard wanted. The rear wheel arches were constructed around the wheels and that leads us to another story that's crucial for the look. The Porsche 996 Hollow Spoke 18-inch wheels were originally fitted to a 996 Turbo in Bernard's extensive Porsche past. He had originally intended to fit them to one of his previous T4s, only to discover that the 11-inch wide rears poked out about five inches beyond the »

The exhaust is topped off by a 'flapper' which, apart from keeping the rain out of the engine, is just one of those pleasingly cool accessories, as are the bespoke sidebars custom made for the Doka

arches! However the Doka project gave him the ideal opportunity to use them, so Ade constructed the 'tubbed' mudguards that rise from the rear deck specifically around these radical rims. The rear deck is protected from the harsh realities of the real world by some astroturf!

Staying at the rear, Ade constructed a square box section crash structure and truck-style mud flaps were fitted, along with rear running lights and hamburger rear-lights. Rear-facing task lights are mounted on top of the rear section of the cab and they sit alongside another Ade Tilly masterpiece, the aluminium truck stack exhaust. The exhaust is topped off by a 'flapper' which, apart from keeping the rain out of the engine, is just one of those pleasingly cool accessories, as are the bespoke sidebars custom made for the Doka.

Up front you'll spot DRL headlight and indicator units from Transporters-R-Us and a Mk1 Golf GTI front splitter. The main central grille has been painted in gloss black whilst the upper bonnet and lower front panel grilles were treated to the same matt yellow as the rest of the bus—completed by Ace Spray in Medway, it's the exact colour and fin-

ish that Caterpillar use on their tractors, so not only does the shade highlight the Doka's lines perfectly, but it's authentic too. Front and rear hazard tape highlights and custom side and rear window graphics complete the exterior look.

Stepping inside, you'll not be shocked to find a few surprises there also, starting with the denim clad seats, continuing the hardwearing industrial theme. The covers were sewn together by Bernard's Nan from some of his old jeans! The dash and door cards have been painted black by and a rusted corrugated iron panel—to keep the tough theme going—tops the dash; the 'iron' is actually a light-

Unique is too small a word for the Dogapillar. Some will love it, while others will not, but what is undoubtedly clear is the level of expertise, engineering, styling, and sheer single-minded conception that has gone into the creation

weight plastic material that has been painted with a rust effect paint, which does the job well. Some more machismo is added with the red pedals and the flash of genius that is the unique T-shaped gear lever, modelled on an explosive detonator plunger. The rest of the interior is intentionally dark, with a black checker cab mat and a stunning black suede headlining that runs right down the A pillars. In the rear the seat—which was missing from the bus—has not been replaced as yet, but the space has been beautifully boxed in and carpeted in black.

Under the bonnet the 2.5 Tdi remains mostly

untouched apart from a full service, overhaul and some belt work, all carried out by Bernard's usual oily bit engineer, Dean Larkins at Larkins Automotive Services, who also lowered the bus to its current pleasing altitude.

In a final flourish Bernard sourced the child's 'Cat' digger for displaying on the rear deck. When it turned up it was in completely the wrong shade, so this too has had the Ace Spray treatment so it was ready to take up its rightful place on the rear deck and complete the overall look.

Unique is too small a word for the Dogapillar. Some will love it, while others will not, but what is undoubtedly clear is the level of expertise, engineering, styling, and sheer single-minded conception that has gone into the creation of this true one-of-a-kind T4. Spectacular! ●

STYLE
& SUBSTANCE

Enroute to testing a Toyota
Hilux Surf 4X4 when you spot a
Volkswagen T4 on the side of the
road for sale, you know it's time to
make the correct decision

📷 : *James Whitlock* 🖹 : *Alan Hayward*

111

112

M at Iles has owned and used a VW bus for a few years now after narrowly avoiding the Toyota route—it's the perfect vehicle to transport his young family around, to supplement his surfing and rugby playing hobbies, and to use in his work as an employment support officer for adults with learning disabilities. Having had his first T4—a gunmetal grey 1.9 panel van he put 75,000 miles on in four years—he started to cast around for a newer T4 to upgrade to.

And as luck would have it, a red Caravelle was thrust under his nose. His partner, Annie—who also works with adults with learning disabilities—came home one night with exciting news of a van for sale. A deal was quickly done and a Tornado Red 2.5 TDi Caravelle Executive that had covered a paltry 52,000 miles was now in their possession. The van had been resting in a garden-based slumber under cover for around three years, but amazingly, all it needed to get it back on the road was an MoT, a quick service and a new battery.

What was clear with with the conversion is that Mat and Annie need a versatile bus: "The van has to be practical, whether I'm using it to take the kids to the beach, take adults with learning difficulties to work, or slotting in the middle row of seats (stored in the garage) so that I can take eight people away on a family holiday. It has to be comfortable too, so

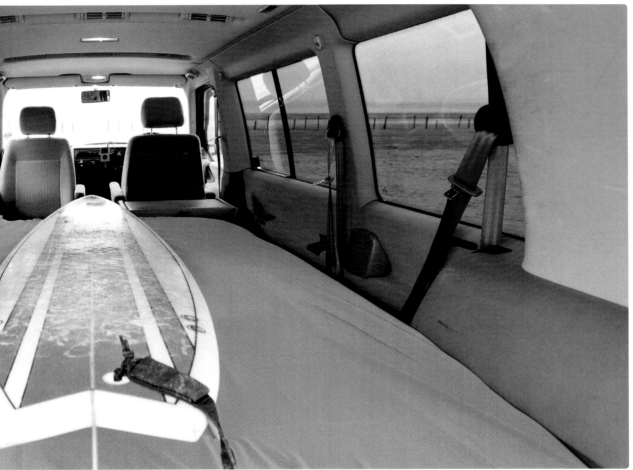

"I don't buy into the whole 'get it so low that I have to plan my routes avoiding speed bumps' or the 'I need 200bhp' thing"

I don't buy into the whole 'get it so low that I have to plan my routes avoiding speed bumps' or the 'I need 200bhp' thing. Having said that, the alloys were a must—driving round on those 15-inch steelies was just too much for me! Initially I put 17-inch Mk5 Golf GTi rims on, until Den, Annie's Dad, kindly donated the 18-inch Borbets that I've got on now."

Other additions to the bus include the kitchen pod made by a full-time fireman/part-time carpenter friend, Ron Tipping, which is interchangeable with the middle row of seats. It has a two-ring gas burner sourced from eBay on top and a two-door cupboard underneath. That's very handy for holidays and surfing trips. The pair came up with the concertina bed together. When the rear seat is »

up it folds into the back and acts as a parcel shelf. When the rear seat is folded flat, it concertinas out to become a bed platform large and strong enough to comfortably support Mat's rugby player frame, Annie, and their two young children as well.

In sleep mode the rear is supported by one central leg and the front by three further legs, all of which are screwed into place on arrival. As the family has grown, extra space was deemed necessary, so a four-berth caravan is now happily towed round by the Caravelle, meaning the clever bed system now gets infrequent use, mainly for quick surf trips and nights away with the lads. Rob Slade, owner Slade Auto Electrical, supplied, fitted and wired up the tow bar for the caravan, having previously installed a new leisure battery well. Rob takes care of all Mat's electrical needs, but Mat does get his hands dirty himself, fitting some locally-sourced side steps and servicing the van every 6,000 miles, including oil and filter change.

Now, like Mat's last bus, this camper gets used!

The bus did 2,500 miles that trip and didn't miss a beat, as well as returning 38mpg, even with a fully loaded roof-box on top

The family drove all through France in 2010, stopping just outside Clermont-Ferrand in the Massif Central for a wedding, before continuing all the way to St Tropez in the South to stay with friends for two weeks. The bus did 2,500 miles that trip and didn't miss a beat, as well as returning 38mpg, even with a fully loaded roof-box on top. While Mat admits a cruise control kit would have been helpful for covering the distance without getting stiff ankles, the responsive T4 was thoroughly enjoyed when driving around the Monte Carlo F1 Grand Prix circuit.

This T4 falls into the category of being fairly stock, but with some subtle alterations added in order to fulfil the varied needs and taste of the owner. This may well be the most apt description for a large number of bus owners; Mat loves his bus, but more importantly, he loves what he can do with his bus. His surf hobby may have led him to bus ownership, but now it's under his skin! ●

BIG BOYS
TOYS

Paul McDougall combined 30-plus years of automotive experience and craftsmanship with his love of VWs of all shapes and sizes to create perfect campervan conversions

📷 : *James Randle* ♟ : *Ian Garrad*

With an automotive heritage that can be traced right back to breaking down and modding Matchbox cars as a child, Paul has always been the hands-on type when it comes to his vehicles. Coupled with his love of the freedom and lifestyle ingrained in bus ownership and the results are a conversion company, where the work is second to none and the buses are made to be used. Briefly dabbling in old school campers, Paul switched tack to a vehicle that is a bit more efficient to convert, with a template that is a bit quicker to turn around, the VW T4. Now in high demand, we come to this particular, rather splendid T4 creation.

The base van is a 1999 2.5 TDi 102bhp that started life as a plain white panel van before Paul resprayed it a cool shade of Ford Vision Blue. The interior is a little different from usual in that it has a side bed, which alters the layout adding a little extra space. Paul had carried out a similar conversion on a T5 some years back along with colour-changing LEDs against minimalist white cabinets, and he wanted to bring some of those elements into this conversion, albeit with a more intimate feel this time. This was achieved with the installation of mica worktops and an unusual material chosen for the headlining »

The black base cloth of the headlining is accented with charcoal coloured insulated carpet lining (including the cab roof), contemporary linoleum floor and black leather upholstery—the detailing on this which features intricate white stitching

that looks almost holographic as it refracts light from the various LEDs built into the ceiling, side step, and even under the worktops. The black base cloth of the headlining is accented with charcoal coloured insulated carpet lining (including the cab roof), contemporary linoleum floor and black leather upholstery—the detailing on which features intricate white stitching. Contrasting all this is a cherry wood veneer on the cabinetry itself, which helps complete the sophisticated interior scheme. In addition to the 12-volt lighting, a Smev hob and Waeco fridge have been installed along with a 240-volt hook-up fueling power sockets and TV points.

The van is just as well presented from the outside, with a set of polished side bars with matching roof rails. The windows have been tinted, while the bumpers have been smoothed and colour-coded, along with the mirrors and door handles. The van has been further modified by a set of DRL Audi-style headlights, and the Audi theme continues with some super cool R8 ten-spoke 18-inch rims, over which the bus has been lowered a further 50mm with the aid of new springs and shocks. The finishing touch was the installation of parking sensors so the new owners could keep that paint pristine.

As mentioned, Paul's buses are made to be used, and this one is no different. The new owner, Mark McGreevy, was very happy when he picked it up, ready for its first run out with the long trip back to Hampshire. Mark came about ordering a build from Paul due to a recommendation by a friend who'd had a camper built by Paul last year. Mark saw his mate's bus and was instantly inspired as to how one would be ideal for his outdoor lifestyle of dog walking, fishing and exploring with the family.

Further to this, having taken early retirement after years of faithful service with the Police Service, Mark wanted a camper that wasn't 'fuddy duddy' as he wasn't ready to embrace the beige. And the sporty look of this super cool camper is exactly right as Mark swaps his blue uniform for this blue bus.

One of the best things for Mark, was being able to have a bespoke vehicle built to his own specific needs. He was able to have lots of input throughout the build, with the floor, lighting design and those epic big Audi wheels all being down to his input. Now that Mark has his freedom and camper in which to enjoy it, what's on the horizon for him and his bus? He explains: "When it comes to getting out and enjoying the new lifestyle, this will certainly do the trick. I'm looking forward to using it for getting out on walks in the forest and walking our three dogs, followed by a relaxing cup of tea in 'Bluebell'— and the hope that my daughters, Olivia and Lily, will enjoy the challenge of camping away from Facebook and television!" If anything will manage such a task, it'll be this T4 and the lifestyle it encapsulates. ●

120

BUMBLE
T

Finding a van on eBay doesn't always turn up sound results, but after putting in a cheeky bid, Ross Martin is clearly a very lucky man

📷 : *Rick Davy* 🖊 : *Alan Hayward*

122

The van in question was originally a panel van of 1999 vintage with a 2.5TDI, 102bhp, ACV unit installed. Previously owned by Kev Hall—a keen dubber and the proprietor of Voodoo Paintworx in Nottinghamshire—the van got its colours and graphics through Kev's love of the Tour de France, based on the famous yellow jersey for a trip over to follow 'Le Tour'. The name, 'Bumble', on the other hand came from Kev's children for altogether more obvious reasons. Since Ross purchased the van most of the signwritten graphics that adorned the bus have been removed, though happily for Kev, the Voodoo Paintworx logo was retained, given that it was deemed to be quite a cool looking skull by Ross and his wife, Natalie.

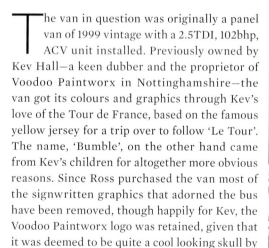

Some other things that were retained from Kev's time with the bus include the evocative two-tone horn that instantly brings Le Tour to mind, and the custom-built black powdercoated roof rack which is perfect for transporting Ross's surf boards and match the black side bars nicely.

As mentioned, Ross found this T4 on eBay not long after his search started. Since collecting the

Unfortunately, after owning the bus for some time, Ross heard the noise all 2.5TDI T4 owners fear the most... the clanking, grinding, banging noise that accompanies a broken cambelt!

bus from Nottinghamshire, it has mostly been used in and around Cornwall where Ross lives. However he too is planning an extensive trip to France, albeit he'll be swapping road bikes for short boards and surfing along the coast. Unfortunately, after owning the bus for some time, Ross heard the noise all 2.5TDI T4 owners

fear the most... the clanking, grinding, banging noise that accompanies a broken cambelt! Upon the RAC coming out to investigate, it was obvious that this T4 was never going to be driving again, the engine having swallowed itself. But Ross took this terrible news and used it as an opportunity.

Contacting the two Steves—Moran and Elson—who run VW Connections based in Truro, Ross explained the problem and dispatched the van to them straight away. A quick look confirmed the diagnosis and Ross feared with Christmas coming up he would be facing a cold, vanless period, but the Steves applied their expertise and excellent » service and announced that it was no problem... they had a 2.5TDI laying about some place they'd planned to put in a Caravelle, but if Ross wanted it, it was his. The deal was struck and the work went ahead, and even more incredible, the work was completed and the van was ready for collection just two days after the boys returned to work post-Christmas, and has performed faultlessly ever since. Expertise, excellent service, and now good friends too.

Since owning Bumble, as well as removing some of the decals—and being forced to go through the engine change ordeal—Ross has added a subtle gloss and matt black bra to the already gloss black bonnet, adding a little extra contrast to the bus. At the front end the grille has now become badge-less to give a little boldness to the lines, while some Audi-style DRL headlights, a VR6 front splitter, and a new side exit exhaust (courtesy of the two Steves again) have been added for a few extra custom touches to Bumble. Stepping inside, the interior has been revamped with a new floor and box unit for the leisure battery and the sub. And if you're wondering about the rock 'n' roll

125

Since owning Bumble, as well as removing some of the decals—and being forced to go through the engine change ordeal—Ross has added a subtle gloss and matt black bonnet bra, adding a little contrast to the bus

bed in the back, it comes courtesy of a Bilbo's conversion originally before it was re-upholstered in some rather eye-catching VW Inca fabric.

And so to the thanks. Ross heaps thanks upon a number of people for their involvement in the creation and his enjoyment of this T4. Firstly, there's Natalie, Ross's wife and surf buddy, who puts up with the lost van hours like so many long suffering partners, not to mention the savings account hit for the purchase in the first place. Then there's Kev Hall, the previous owner and customiser who in many ways helped shape this van into what it is today. Scott Tacchi, a friend who help Ross out during the cambelt escapade, and the two Steves of VW Connections, who turned everything back to normal again. The First and Last Dub Club, based in southwest Cornwall who in Ross's opinion keep the Cornish scene alive and kicking. Anna Lazzarino, who at short notice got out of bed early and kindly opened up The Mount Hawke Skate Park, for the photo shoot. And lastly, Daisy the Beagle, loyal companion, lover of long walks, and van appreciator-in-chief. ●

Pre-facelift T5a Multivan.

THE VAN THAT DRIVES
LIKE A CAR!

T5: 2003–present day

: *David Eccles*

ntroduced in 2003, the T5 quickly established itself as a market leader continuing the tradition of the VW Transporter as delivery van, people carrier and, for the first time, a VW-built camper. As well as featuring the latest trends and innovations in automotive engineering, design and technology, the T5 is bigger and roomier—15mm longer, 50mm higher and 64mm wider with an impressive carrying capacity of 5.8 cubic metres. At launch in 2003 both petrol and diesel engine options were offered, but from 2010 the range was limited to two-litre diesel only variants, delivering from 84PS up to 180PS and using common-rail technology instead of injectors. Body styling softened the square commercial van look with rounded corners and edges, while the different engine, body, and cab design options and combinations meant an incredible 375 variants

were offered by the factory, including the successful 4Motion all-wheel drive, first introduced on the T4.

But what really makes the T5 stand out is the way it drives. It simply does not feel like a commercial; and the addition of options such as six-speed gearbox or DSG (automatic gearbox) make driving both effortless and pleasurable. Whilst the commercial models are a bit more spartan in terms of standard equipment, a full range of options is available to alter styling and comfort, including colour-coded bumpers instead of the black commercial versions. The top of the range Caravelle models are geared to the needs of a modern family with a floor-mounted rail system to slide seats or position a table and come with a full range of extras as standard, and for complete luxury, the Business Class Caravelle has everything—no wonder it is the favourite tour vehicle for the likes of Robbie Williams!

2013 T5b (Facelift) California.

In September 2013 VW launched a luxury special edition of the humble pick-up, resurrecting the name Tristar from the T3 version.

Home is where you park it!

Off-road fun in a 4Motion (4WD) Mulitivan.

T5 'Facelift'

In 2010 the T5 received a front end makeover, with the aim being to more closely resemble models in the VW car range. Restyled with a sloping nose and daytime running lights, new grill and bumper styling, new rear light clusters and redesigned cab and dash, and coupled with the new two-litre engines and safety improvements, the Facelift has continued to sell exceptionally well.

VW's first camper

With the T5 also came a first for Volkswagen—the introduction of its own factory-built camper, the California. Having severed its ties with West-falia in 2002 when it was taken over by a rival conglomerate, VW set up a dedicated assembly plant in Limmer (a suburb of Hannover) where the Californias are hand assembled from supplied components. Based on a Caravelle and featuring an electric powered aluminium elevating roof, faced aluminium cabinets, an outside table stored as a side panel in the sliding door, two camping chairs stored in a zip compartment on the inside of the tailgate, blinds, swivelling cab seats, sink, fridge, hob and sleeping for four (the roof bed is huge!), the California has established a dedicated

What really makes the T5 stand out is the way it drives; it simply does not feel like a commercial

following. RHD models did not appear until 2005, and the UK version comes with impressive equipment and range of options as standard helping it become the UK's biggest selling campervan. A weekend version, known as the Beach, with manual roof and seats rather than a camping interior, is also very popular as a family MPV.

The biggest growth in the T5 camper market, however, is undoubtedly the rise of small bespoke companies offering tailor made, one-stop shop conversions catering for all budgets. Elevating roofs, side windows, individually designed interiors to suit your own lifestyle and taste—these small conversion companies offer an outstanding personal service and many go on to become much admired show winners as well as family campers! VW have also re-established ties with Westfalia, and in 2012 a high-top T5 camper called the Club Joker was introduced, while 2014 saw the launch of an elevating roof version.

With a worldwide sales figure already hitting 1.7 million by 2013, the T5 has continued to prove the vehicle of choice for both commercial and leisure use. ●

128

GOING
DUTCH

This is the story of a Dutchman,
a rare bus, some serial modding,
and an invitation to one of Europe's
best tuning shows

📷 : Mick Kok 🗎 : Alan Hayward

When you're invited to show your bus at
the Torino Tuning Expo in Italy—an
exhibition that draws industry leaders,
component manufacturers and customisers together to display their latest creations—you can be
pretty sure you've created a very cool bus. Dutchman, Dave Crijns, certainly has. Dave hails from
Maastricht in the Netherlands, which is home

130

Dave acquired the bus back in December of 2011, trading in both a VW Caddy and a private car to buy a T5 and gain a little more space

to the family business specialising in tyres, Crijns Banden. And having been around the family business all his life, he very naturally developed a keen interest in all things automotive from a very young age, which was nurtured and matured into an interest in the huge European tuning scene.

Dave acquired the bus back in December of 2011, trading in both a VW Caddy and a private car to buy a T5 and gain a little more space. The one he found was a fairly stock long wheel base that looked a tidy Kombi in 'Off-Road' Grey Metallic, with twin sliders, fitted with the 2.5 TDI PD engine. What originally marked this bus out from the norm, however, was that it came in 'T Edition' trim. Not available in the UK, the T Edition had—amongst other things— leather captain's seats up front and similarly clad Kombi seats in the back, a chrome grille, which Dave has subsequently changed, 16-inch 'Miyato' alloys, Multivan rear lights, bumpers and parking sensors, plus a liberal sprinkling of T Edition

131

Dave made a few adjustments and the result is a perfectly reliable T5, now with a staggering PK figure of 220!

badges and logos throughout. When Dave got the van it had already been tuned to produce around 180 PK or paardenkracht (Dutch for 'horsepower'). Now all that horsepower sounds great, but the whole thing had been tuned in the wrong way, according to Dave. The net effect of this was that two days before he was due to go on holiday the turbo blew out. Luckily, Dave was able to replace it himself and still got away on time, but right after they got back the replacement went the same way as its predecessor. So a more satisfactory solution was sought and the turbo was replaced for a second time. Dave made a few adjustments and the result is a perfectly reliable T5, now with a staggering PK figure of 220! »

But Dave's van mods didn't stop there. Firstly to achieve the stance he wanted, he fitted V-Maxx coilover suspension as the basis for his air-ride system, which came from Kean Suspensions in Evergem, just outside Ghent, in Belgium. It's a four-way kit that's been fitted using eight millimetre lines and the result couldn't be any cooler, or indeed any lower. Then there are the wheels. Out went the 16-inch T Edition Volkswagen Miyato alloys and in came their replacements—wrapped in Pirelli P Zero 245/30/22 rubber from the family store, they are 22-inch Range Rover Sport wheels. The trouble is they didn't fit until Dave did some heavy modding, taking a little bit out of the back of the wheel where it bolts up to get the offset down so that they would fit under the arches... the bolts needed some adjustment too.

New rear side windows have been added to the mix. Whilst, the rear lights have been smoked, the front fog-lights have been given a golden hue. The front grille is now badgeless and the bonnet has been filled so no sign of the VW roundel remains up front providing a smooth finish. Chrome side

It almost drives like a regular car, but with lots of extra space. When I go out with my mates, they always want to go in my ride

steps and a few decals complete the exterior look. Inside an R36 Passat steering wheel sits atop the steering column, lending some OEM style.

So what does Dave think of his bus now? After all it's hardly 'stock' anymore. "I like that it feels a lot sportier, more sporty than a Mercedes Vito for instance. It almost drives like a regular car, but with lots of extra space. When I go out with my mates, they always want to go in my ride. I think because it looks awesome and it's much easier when we have to take stuff with us. I love that people actually stop to take photos, which makes me very proud to drive it." And drive it he does, making the 2,500km trip to Turin for the Torino Tuning Expo, and it didn't miss a single beat.●

LIFE'S A
BEACH

The VW T5 California Beach was launched to a healthy amount of fanfare. And looking at the versatility, finish and specification of the stock bus, it's easy to see why when test driving one for a weekend working at Camper Jam

📷🎞 : *Owen Moran* **Additional photography**: *VW press*

Delivered looking spotless and factory fresh with less than 3,000 miles on the clock, it was barely run in. Climbing into the armchair-style front seats you are instantly rewarded with a high driving position and view from this highly distinctive and classy Sunny Yellow camper. And having driven many a T5 before I was pleasantly surprised at quite how well the 2.0-litre TDi BlueMotion fared, pulling effortlessly through each of the six gears to reach a comfortable cruising speed.

Inside, the modern dash and clear display panel gives you the impression of driving an executive car, while the multi-function steering wheel puts radio, mobile phone, and even cruise controls at your fingertips—the addition of iPod/iPhone adapter cable, neatly tucked away in the glove box, also allows for full synchronization with your device. All too often driving a large vehicle can have its downsides when it comes to parking, but luckily the Beach was fitted with the extra of full surround parking sensors to make the »

task entirely straight-forward. The interior layout of the Beach means that you can comfortably carry four adult passengers and copious amounts of equipment, but it's the versatility that sets it aside. There are many layout options with the rear bench seat on rails so it can be easily moved forwards and back to accommodate larger items in the boot area, or simply to bring rear passengers and driver closer, handy if you're carrying young children. There's also a practical folding table stowed in the sliding door that can be attached both inside the van and outside, which combines with the two folding chairs cleverly tucked away in the tailgate for alfresco dining. Other factory interior layout options include a full-width three-seat bench and additional swivel seats providing seven-seat possibilities. The interior storage chest fitted on this model meant you could store/hide any number of items quickly, and the addition of a sliding compartment under the bench seat means larger items can be stowed out of harm's way too.

Cruising to Camper Jam was an enjoyable drive, and once there it was time to set up 'Camp Beach'. With a tent set up alongside the camper for family overflow and our pet dog, and equipment like a buggy and the usual cooking paraphernalia unloaded, it was time to transform the bus from a transporter into a home. This is where the

Beach's clever use of space really works, with both the two front captain's seats swivelling to create a sitting room-style set-up. Next the roof, which goes up in a matter of seconds thanks to its use of gas struts that kick in almost as soon as you unhook the securing clips—this roof has to be one of the best in the business, not least as it still incorporates the superb slatted base and comfy and roomy six-foot-six double bed. For night reading, there is a handy 12-volt socket for a flexible halogen reading light, however there's no window, so you can only get extra daylight and fresh air via the flyscreen panels in the sides. When not in use as a bed the base of the roof also lifts using gas struts to give the lounge area a superb amount of headroom, allowing even the six-foot-plus of us to move around at ease. Downstairs in the rear, the bench-seat folds flat, converting to a two-berth full-width bed. With the beds sorted and the Fiamma-style roll-out awning up, Camp Beach was complete. Spending

This is where the Beach's clever use of space really works, with both the two front captain's seats swivelling to create a sitting room-style set-up

the three days working at Camper Jam, helping organise the club camping area and the smooth running of the show and shine, before soaking up the atmosphere and fun with my family at the event, meant three long, tiring days in the beautiful Weston Park, equal parts rewarding and exhausting. So it was a most welcome relief to get back to Camp Beach at the end of each day and with little effort, close the integrated pull-down blinds for the side and rear windows, place the pop-up covers for the front windows, and crawl into a very comfy and warm bed. All in all, this vehicle performed excellently with minimal fuss and the utmost comfort. And with wide ranging specs and set ups available, it's easy to see why sticking stock can be a great decision.●

HOME FROM
HOME

Working in a job that required a lot of travel around the south of England—and all the hotel bills that go with it—Mike made the very wise decision to build himself his own hotel on wheels...

📷🖥 : *Andrew Thompson*

This isn't Mike's first van, he had owned a T5 before which was mainly used for commuting; he had carried out some general modifications over a number of years on said van, giving him a taste of what could be achieved when he finally took the plunge on a new dream project bus. And with plenty of commuting time to think, along with some help from the guys over at Vanworx, his dream became reality. After the slow evolution of his last van, Mike wanted his next one to be a finished project from the first turn of the key. Speaking to Dave and Dan at Vanworx in Portland about what he really wanted and needed from a van, Mike's plans grew and grew into the idea of building a fully fitted camper with all the trimmings and then some! When Mike ordered his van it was a com- »

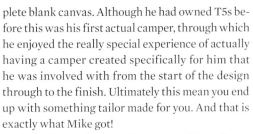

plete blank canvas. Although he had owned T5s before this was his first actual camper, through which he enjoyed the really special experience of actually having a camper created specifically for him that he was involved with from the start of the design through to the finish. Ultimately this mean you end up with something tailor made for you. And that is exactly what Mike got!

The build was based on Vanworx's 'Slipper' conversion, albeit with a few tweaks to suit Mike's tastes and needs. The main unit was manufactured as one piece to strengthen the build—because Mike's van has sliding doors on either side there is nowhere to attach the front part of the 'galley' unit. Mike explained: "I wanted the twin doors so I could use the offside slide door for storage of the gas and water bottles. I can also fit the table in this side which leaves me with lots of valuable space inside the back of the bus to use for all of my work tools."

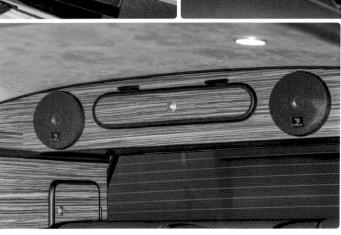

After the slow evolution of his last van, Mike wanted his next one to be a finished project from the first turn of the key. And that's exactly what he got!

Mike's previous van was black, and having owned that for seven years he fancied the Candy White for a change. As for the furniture inside, that's where his wife came to help—it's a relatively new finish in the Vanworx range, but as soon as she saw it, she knew that's what it had to be. Originally opting for white stitching in the leather seats to match the paintwork, Mike ended up going for the Bentley-style diamond stitching with double red stitch, which really sets off the cabinetry beautifully. But the most important thing about the conversion was that the guys at Vanworx really went that extra »

Mike has the perfect rolling hotel for weekday nights away from home, as well as a great weekend camper for his family

mile. When you're spending the kind of money conversions take, you expect the best. And as Mike explained, it's refreshing to go to a company that's so conscious about their product that they tell you when they don't think something will look right, but rather suggest the alteration that can make all the difference. And looking at the end result, you really get your money's worth from the impressive end result.

The original spec list for the vehicle was already impressive, but the completed vehicle spec is something else. The camper has had around a 100mm-plus drop on a set of Bilstein coilovers to get it nice and low to the ground. Then H&R anti-roll bars were fitted to stiffen it up and it's now rolling on a set of 20-inch Autec rims with 275/35 tyres along with a Milltek exhaust system and a Sportline body kit all finished off in the Candy White paint. Inside you have the full leather diamond-stitched interior. Up front a Kenwood double din stereo has been installed with a reversing camera on the back of the bus. A Golf R multi-functional steering wheel was also installed with full working paddle shift systems. In the back, red mood lights were installed along with white LED lights. The gas and water bottles have all been hidden away, but are easily accessible from the sliding door.

Finally, with the bed, sink, fridge and safe under the front seats, Mike has the perfect rolling hotel for weekday nights away from home, as well as a great weekend camper for his family—and now expeditions further afield can be tackled too, with a family road trip through France on the cards. Next up is the addition of a pop-top roof for added space, but in the meantime the stealthy look outside combined with the fully-fitted camper interior is just right. ●

A GERMAN
LESSON

It's a rare thing to come across a custom built doka,
and rarer still to find one that looks like it could have
rolled out of the VW factory...

📷 : *James Northcott* 🖂 : *Alan Hayward*

Designed and built in The Truro Alloy Centre, Richard Clayton—who has a string of stunning show cars and magazine featured VWs to his name—used his expert knowledge and eye for detail, while utilising the facilities up in Brighouse, West Yorkshire, to develop this epic doka to use as his daily driver. This doka has been created from a white LWB van fitted with a drop-sided, tipping-load bed. With the bed discarded, a double cab chassis van remained, onto which the back half of the van was fabricated using panels from a crashed and trashed LWB panel van—the sliding door was welded up and smoothed, the side panels cut down, and at the rear, the doors have been retained and cut down helping achieve the unique look. Unique is certainly the word, »

Out back, the doka's load area is yet another work of art. Richard spent £2,500 on teak completing the task of fabricating a deck that looks like it has come from a luxury yacht

both in concept and execution. This is how VW should make them!

Taking a closer look at the colour, you may be surprised to know it's from the Ford Focus range. However the apple hue works great on this bus with the lightness in shade allowing you to appreciate the swage lines and bodywork details to the full. The use of black as an accent colour, from the Limo tints and door handles, through to the gloss black painted bonnet panel and ABT grill, helps create an even more distinctive look than the bus already has, and continues with black detailing on the Audi R8-style light that helps give the front a modern, crisp look when combined with the modded Caravelle bumper set-up. Behind the new bumper and light combination nestles a far from standard 2.5 TDI-PD engine that has been fettled, by means of an intercooler, custom exhaust system, and a comprehensive remap, to produce an eye-watering 230bhp (up from the base of 174bhp).

Out back, the doka's load area is yet another work of art. Richard spent £2,500 on teak completing the task of fabricating a deck that looks like it has come from a luxury yacht. A trap door was

147

Inside, you will not be disappointed to learn, the attention to detail and quality continues, providing a fabulous place to spend some time

added to give access to the lower, enclosed (and consequently more secure) load space. And to give an idea of scale, the upper bed is roughly six-foot by five-foot which means lots of useable space both above and below deck. The whole bus sits 80mm down on coilovers and runs on a set of 9.5x22-inch Dotz dressed with 265/30/R/22 Continentals. These super-bling items whilst not to everyone's taste, suit this doka to a T, complementing the rest of the spectacular exterior nicely. And on the road this set-up is spot on as well, with the bus being stupidly quick but with enough grip to compen-

sate for the added hp and torque the engineering provide. The ride is, well, it's pretty much what you would expect from a lowered bus running on conveyor belt tyres... it's a bit hardcore, but again, you'd expect nothing less on this bus.

Inside, you will not be disappointed to learn, the attention to detail and quality continues, providing a fabulous place to spend some time. Up front you'll find a pair of über-cool, red leather Audi TT seats, electrically motivated of course; in the back, the one-piece bench seat has been recovered to match the front pair, as have the door cards. And to finish the whole thing off, even the custom cab carpets (front and rear) are edged in red.

Inside and out, this doka looks as though it was meant to be. If anything, it looks like the embodiment of a concept car drawn up, not in Truro or Brighouse, but in Wolfsburg or Hannover. So the real lesson to take from this is should be for Volkswagen themselves. ●

THE NEW
WAVE

When Emily and Mike of New Wave
Custom Conversions finished their new
demo van in 2014 it would have been
rude not to go and take a look...

📷🎥 : *Andrew Thompson*

Dropping into their workshop in Pontyclun, South Wales, for the annual unveiling of the New Wave show vehicle, you will always feel like you are going to see something special, and as usual they didn't disappoint with their latest top of the line T5. And to say New Wave have pedigree is an understatement; last year's van with it's traditional 'lux' interior, full air ride and 3SDM rims, spent the summer being welcomed at different shows around the country and perhaps some shows that as van owners you may not think of visiting—the 2013 demo van won trophies at both Edition 38 and at the Prept Vs Players showdown, and gained some really positive feedback along the way.

Turning attention to the 2014 van, it arrived in the workshop as a T30 Highline panel van, a two-litre TDI with 140bhp in deep black metallic paint—it wasn't really a colour they usually go for with campers, but it was perfect on their new Luxury 'Beach' demo, giving off that stealth OEM look with all of the Sportline exterior additions that were added during the build. And it has to be said, while black can be time consuming to keep clean, when this camper is shined up it looks amazing and well worth the effort.

NWCC only complete the conversion specifications outlined on their website after taking the decision in January 2012 to set up for production rather than complete custom work. Each conversion layout has been designed, developed and perfected over the last five-plus years, and with that in mind, NWCC make sure to offer as many conversion layouts as possible to allow customers to utilise the T5 as best they can, to suit their individual needs. One configuration which was needed, was housing a three-person seat/bed system, as well as cooking facilities and a fridge. They were looking to offer a conversion which would be perfect for not only day-to-day use, the school run and work, but also suitable for the spontaneous overnight trip—the Luxury 'Beach' conversion is a perfect example of this.

Something that is always a concern when converting a van is space. Many people require high levels of versatility when it comes to the interior, wanting it to be pristine and spacious, but also with the option of accommodating more rear passengers, which led to the creation of the new

We were looking to offer a conversion which would be perfect for not only day-to-day use, the school run and work, but also suitable for the spontaneous overnight trip

layout that incorporates the RIB150. The seats in both the front and back have been upholstered by Lee, the extremely talented in-house upholster at New Wave Custom Conversions using an Auto Calf grained leather with a golden contrasting topstitch—and as with any demo vehicle, they aim to showcase something different, in this case, the twin stitch, fluted and perforated centre panels. The shape of the units has been designed to not only allow the RIB to fully extend, but also house a CAN single sink and cooker. Although the sink isn't as wide as others available on the market, and at first glance you may think not the ideal choice, it is however rather deep, making it very practical. The headlining has been finished in Alcantara, with the rear in slatted panels. There is a drop-down Alpine 10.2-inch monitor which has the »

153

built-in gameport allowing you to connect game consoles, video cameras or DVD players quickly and easily, so those long journeys aren't so boring for your passengers in the back!

The NWCC team are huge VW enthusiasts and strongly believe no look is better than, or can compare to, the OEM factory finish. That's why the exterior has been fitted with several Sportline accessories, including sidebars, 40mm lowering springs and 18-inch alloys. On the back to continue the OEM theme is a VW tailgate bike rack that can carry up to four bikes, ideal for the whole family. And speaking of which, even though this van conversion started out as a show vehicle, thankfully it was quickly snapped up by a local family who are all keen cyclists planning to use the van as it should be. So while you may not see this on the NWCC stand at shows this year, you never know, you may spot it in the show and shine field with the new owners or next to a cycle track or campsite near you! Otherwise, keep an eye out for New Wave's next instalment. ●

The NWCC team are huge VW enthusiasts and strongly believe no look is better than, or can compare to, the OEM factory finish

154

T4&5 BITE-SIZE
BUYER'S GUIDE

155

Now that you've chosen the water-cooled route to a modernity, make sure you know what you're getting and what to avoid while selecting your bus with our essential guide

📷 : *Various* 🖊 : *Fergus McShane*

I f you are reading this, then you'll probably either have already dabbled in VW buses, or are about to. The following is not a comprehensive 'How to' guide, but rather an overview of what you can expect to come across when searching for or converting a bus, and an outline of some things you will find yourself choosing between. Options are varied and extensive, but opting for a VW bus in the first place means you have already chosen well.

Designed to fit into a standard in size parking space, the VW bus footprint is not that different to a large family saloon, but it has an an elevated driving position that makes a big difference on the road, coupled with the added reliability and power from modern manufacturing.

For more information on the T4 and T5 model variants launched over the years, turn to the History of the T4 and T5 on page 98 and 126 respectively. As an overview, the T4 comes in short and long wheelbase, panel van, Kombi, Multivan and Westfalia camper conversion. A facelift model introduced a more passenger car front end look, while there are options for roof height, pop-top and interior specifications. With T5s a few more models arrived, from the basic panel van, up through Kombi to Sportline, Caravelle and the top-end California model. »

Engine options

There are a range of engine options available for the T4 and T5, from economic 1.9 diesels delivering under 90bhp, to the mighty 3.2-litre petrol VR6s with over 230bhp. It's worth considering the use when choosing—day vans can cruise comfortably with a smaller engine, whereas the added weight of a full camper conversion can require a bit more pull from a larger unit. You can generally tell the type from the badge. On the T4, the 2.5-litre engine provides ample torque and good economy with three variants: blue 'i' on the TDi badge delivered 87bhp; silver 'i' 102bhp; and the more rare red 'i', 149bhp.

On the T5 you find just as much choice—the 2.0 and 2.5 TDi are popular, but the petrol FSi is also a good option. Early T5s return much the same as T4s—around 83bhp for the 1.9 up to 174bhp on the 2.5. 2010 saw a switch to improved 2.0-litre engines offering the top end bhp, while a greener BlueMotion option came available offering 112bhp.

If you are transitioning from a T1–T3 VW bus to a modern bus, you will find the gears the biggest jump with both the T4 and 5 offering smooth and efficient control. However it should be noted that the automatics available, are a bit more susceptible to breakdown and can be a costly fix. As with everything mechanical, regular checks and maintenance is vital.

IT'S WORTH CONSIDERING THE USE WHEN CHOOSING—DAY VANS CAN CRUISE COMFORTABLY WITH A SMALLER ENGINE

Camper converting

Looking at individual examples of campervan conversions will give a great overview of what to think of when converting a van yourself. There's lots of info out there and many companies and people who can give invaluable advice.

Firstly, your budget is going to determine the bus and build you go for. The genuine Westfalia California is an incredible machine, but the high price is prohibitive, as is the LHD set-up if you're UK-based. However, British conversions sell for nearly as much because of the demand for RHD. Some convertors of note are the Germans, Dehler, Carthago, Weinberg and Reimo, or in Britain, the likes of Autohomes, Autosleeper, Komet, Bilbos and Danbury.

The more common route is to buy a solid donor vehicle and go down the DIY road with many installation kits available, or to approach one of the smaller bespoke converters, of which there are many with varied levels of quality output. This takes planning and time, but it's a great way to get something practical and modern, built new and tailored to how you plan on using it. The Reimo catalogue is an excellent starting point offering access to proper crash tested seats and seatbelts, as well as their huge product line.

There are many DIY conversions or part conversions out there for sale. The best advice on how to approach these is meticulously... unless you can confirm the build quality, material quality and workmanship, you are taking a risk. For example, lowering the suspension and aftermarket alloys are commonplace, but if done incorrectly can make the van dangerous and uninsurable.

158

AS WITH PURCHASING ANY MODERN VEHICLE, HPI CHECKS CAN BE INVALUABLE TO MAKE SURE THERE'S NOTHING LURKING IN THE VEHICLE'S HISTORY YOU SHOULD BE AWARE OF

Know what you're getting

You will find that, aside from buses for sale at VW shows and all the regular VW fan websites, the main port of call for buying T4s and 5s is eBay. While you can turn up a bargain if you are patient and refrain from spontaneous purchases, it can also result in a driveway money pit. As there are quite a number of variants across 4s and 5s—from Caravelles and Multivans to Shuttles and Transporter Kombis—make sure you know the model you are buying is the right one for you and that the spec matches the model.

Additionally, if rear seats/furniture and windows have been added during a conversion, check where and when work was carried out, but most importantly if you'll be using the rear seats while in transit, check that they're crash tested and properly fitted. If buying a full camper conversion, check the electrics and gas appliances work and have a regu-

lar service history. As with purchasing any modern vehicle, HPI checks can be invaluable to make sure there's nothing lurking in the vehicle's history you should be aware of. And as always, don't buy before inspecting. More often than you'd think—and exacerbated by the fact that modern buses sell so quickly once listed and priced correctly—the temptation is there to rush into purchases, ultimately to be left disappointed. Patience is key.

PRICE GUIDE

Similarly to buying a 'classic' VW, cost fluctuates massively throughout the marque. And again, the cost you'll pay varies throughout the year and follows sporadic trends. So you are probably best to establish your budget before deciding whether to go to one of the many VW-dedicated convertors for a completed van (often with the option to have a suitable van sourced for you for a little extra expense), to go direct to VW for something from the current stock, or to look around, purchase and uprate a bare shell van. The latter option leaves much of the budgeting up to you, which can be good and bad—budgets can grow and grow when you add up things like installing windows, a pop-top, R&R bed,

new electrics, but it can also be a more personally fulfilling way to work.

As a rough guide for T4 prices (as a bare shell), you can source a decent-to-good early '90s T4 for as little as £1,000; with a later higher spec T4 Caravelle or Multivan for upwards of £10,000. For a Westfalia model or a professionally built aftermarket camper, you can expect to pay anywhere between £5,000–£25,000 depending on age and spec.

On the T5 front, newer is costlier, but with an ex-builder's van you can find a project bus for £5,000–£7,000. For Shuttle and Caravelle variants, £9,000 will be the lower limit, and you can pay anything up to £35,000-plus for a luxury, well-maintained later model. And similarly to T4s, you can expect the fully converted campers and high-spec current models direct from VW to cost that bit more.

Ultimately, whatever your budget and whatever you buy, choose carefully, plan meticulously, and you will be out there soaking up the modern VW bus lifestyle in no time. Enjoy! ●

Friendly & fun, a family VW bus event for all types

Camper Jam '15

Weston Park, Shropshire

3-5 July 2015

TICKETS ON SALE NOW

For more information call 01244 881895 Ext. 523

www.camperjam.com

MOTOR INSURANCE THAT PROTECTS YOUR PASSION.

Because we know you're not just insuring a car, you're insuring a lifestyle.

OUR POLICIES CAN INCLUDE:
- FREE MOTOR LEGAL EXPENSES
- FREE MODIFICATIONS COVER
- OPTION TO RETAIN SALVAGE
- 24 HOUR HOMESTART BREAKDOWN COVER (UK AND EU)
- AGREED VALUE INSURANCE

CALL HIC FOR A FREE QUOTE

0800 085 9275

hertsinsurance.com